FRANKLIN FOER

Franklin Foer is a national correspondent for the *Atlantic* and a fellow at the New America Foundation. For seven years, he edited the *New Republic* magazine. He is the author of *How Football Explains the World*, which has been translated into 27 languages and won a National Jewish Book Award. He has been called one of America's 'most influential liberal journalists' by the *Daily Beast*. He lives in Washington, D.C.

ALSO BY FRANKLIN FOER

How Football Explains the World

As Editor

Jewish Jocks (with Marc Tracy)
Insurrections of the Mind

FRANKLIN FOER

World Without Mind

Why Google, Amazon, Facebook and
Apple Threaten Our Future

VINTAGE

1 3 5 7 9 10 8 6 4 2

Vintage
20 Vauxhall Bridge Road,
London SW1V 2SA

Vintage is part of the Penguin Random House group of companies
whose addresses can be found at global.penguinrandomhouse.com

Copyright © Franklin Foer 2017

Franklin Foer has asserted his right to be identified as the author of this
Work in accordance with the Copyright, Designs and Patents Act 1988

First published in Vintage in 2018
First published in hardback by Jonathan Cape in 2017

penguin.co.uk/vintage

A CIP catalogue record for this book is available from the British Library

ISBN 9781784707347

Printed and bound in Great Britain by Clays Ltd, Elcograf S.p.A.

Penguin Random House is committed to a sustainable future
for our business, our readers and our planet. This book is made
from Forest Stewardship Council® certified paper.

TO BERT FOER

Ardent Trustbuster, Gentle Father

"The glow of one warm thought is to me worth more than money."

Thomas Jefferson, 1773

CONTENTS

SECTION I
THE MONOPOLISTS OF MIND

SECTION II
WORLD WITHOUT MIND

SECTION III
TAKE BACK THE MIND

Preface to the British Edition

Back so many years ago, I spent a year at Oxford, that movie set where young American anglophiles briefly acquire ersatz accents and vacation their way through a year of binge drinking.

MI had just turned twenty, still with a proclivity to pimples, and I had never been so intellectually impressionable. No book will ever have the magnetic force of the tomes that I discovered that amid my post-adolescent wanderings through Blackwell's bookshop and the college library. I read with a fervor and abandon that I have fruitlessly tried to recapture ever since.

One of the greatest discoveries were the broadsheets and tabloids splayed on the floor and couches of the college's Junior Common Room. They were bulging, gorgeous piles, wondrous in their diversity of styles, shapes, and colors. Sitting for hours each afternoon with the inexhaustible papers, I came to realize the stodginess and bland respectability of the press back home.

This was the mid-nineties, and I couldn't quite believe the bounty. Freed from the fetters of objectivity that constrained the *New York Times* and *Washington Post*, the papers wrote about the world with panache, joy and force. British politics began to fascinate me as I watched the papers compete for scoops, which appeared with stunning regularity. The coverage of books and movies was exhilarating, both serious and gossipy: the sort of respect for objects of art that occasionally takes the form of disrespect.

I have returned to London nearly every year since. In Britain, you don't need an outsider to tell you about the fate of your press. But the shriveling of British media has broken my heart. With every visit, I could feel that the papers weighed less, contained fewer pages than the last time. The decline in quality of reporting and prose was as easily discernable as the shedding of physical mass.

There are many explanations for Brexit and the rise of Donald Trump. But there's one source of our woes that seems transcendent to me: the poor quality of information consumed by our citizenry. This is a book about the forces in the world that have spurred confusion, conformism, and, sad to say, stupidity.

Once upon a time, we thought of globalization of culture as the export of Hollywood and American television. Snobs berated my country for its role in unleashing these irresistible forces, for reshaping the world in our own image. And the snobs weren't entirely wrong. But those criticisms also feel a bit quaint compared to the current iteration of cultural globalization. This time homogenization masquerades as something else—it gives the illusion of personal control and personal liberation. But that illusion merely makes it far more pernicious than anything that has come before. What I'm describing, and will spend the coming pages describing, is the way in which companies like Facebook, Amazon, Google, and Apple are remaking the world for the worse.

There are many plausible reasons for the waning of the British press, for the sorry state of the informational ecosystem. But it's also the victim of forces from beyond its shores. The British press was a product of a national culture, an indigenous creation. It reflected virtues and foibles that could never translate to any other place in the world. Like France's wine or Switzerland's timepieces, the press was Britain's great native product. Sadly, that localism has been drowned, a drowning that occurred slowly but was finally forced under by Facebook and Google.

This is a plotline, of course, replicated in nearly every nation, except for a few staunch resisters. Still, I mourn Britain's loss—it fills me with nostalgia and sadness—although I hope you won't give up so easily. The defeat of higher ideals is hardly final. I hope to persuade you that another course is still possible.

PROLOGUE

UNTIL RECENTLY, it was easy to define America's most widely known corporations. Any third grader could describe their essence. Exxon sells oil; McDonald's makes hamburgers; Walmart is a place to buy stuff. This is no longer so. The ascendant monopolies of today aspire to encompass all of existence. Some of these companies have named themselves for their limitless aspirations. Amazon, as in the most voluminous river on the planet, has a logo that points from A to Z; Google derives from googol, a number (1 followed by 100 zeros) that mathematicians use as shorthand for unimaginably large quantities.

Where do these companies begin and end? Larry Page and Sergey Brin founded Google with the mission of organizing all knowledge, but that proved too narrow. Google now aims to build driverless cars, manufacture phones, and conquer death. Amazon was once content being "the everything store," but now produces television shows, designs drones, and powers the cloud. The most ambitious tech companies—throw Facebook, Microsoft, and Apple into the mix—are in a race to become our "personal assistant." They want to wake us in the morning, have their artificial intelligence software guide us through the day, and never quite leave our sides. They aspire to become the repository for precious and private items, our calendar and contacts, our photos and documents. They intend for us to unthinkingly turn to them for information and entertainment, while they build unabridged catalogs of our intentions and aversions. Google Glass and the Apple Watch prefigure the day when these companies implant their artificial intelligence within our bodies.

More than any previous coterie of corporations, the tech monopolies aspire to mold humanity into their desired image of it. They believe that they have the opportunity to complete the long merger between man and machine—to redirect the trajectory of human evolution. How do I know this? Such suggestions are fairly commonplace in Silicon Valley, even if much of the tech press is too obsessed with covering the latest product launch to take much notice of them. In annual addresses and townhall meetings, the founding fathers of these companies often make big, bold pronouncements about human nature—a view of human nature that they intend to impose on the rest of us.

There's an oft-used shorthand for the technologist's view of the world. It is assumed that libertarianism dominates Silicon Valley, which isn't wholly wrong. High-profile devotees of Ayn Rand can be found there. But if you listen hard to the titans of tech, that's not the worldview that emerges. In fact, it is something much closer to the opposite of a libertarian's veneration of the heroic, solitary individual. The big tech companies believe we're fundamentally social beings, born to collective existence. They invest their faith in the network, the wisdom of crowds, collaboration. They harbor a deep desire for the atomistic world to be made whole. By stitching the world together, they can cure its ills. Rhetorically, the tech companies gesture toward individuality—to the empowerment of the "user"—but their worldview rolls over it. Even the ubiquitous invocation of users is telling, a passive, bureaucratic description of us.

The big tech companies—the Europeans have charmingly, and correctly, lumped them together as GAFA (Google, Apple, Facebook, Amazon)—are shredding the principles that protect individuality. Their devices and sites have collapsed privacy; they disrespect the value of authorship, with their hostility to intellectual property. In the realm of economics, they justify monopoly with their well-articulated belief that competition undermines our pursuit of the common good and ambitious goals. When it comes to the most central tenet of individualism—free will—the tech companies have a different way. They hope to automate the choices, both large and small, that we make as we float through the day. It's their algorithms that suggest the news we read, the goods we buy, the path we travel, the friends we invite into our circle.

It's hard not to marvel at these companies and their inventions, which often make life infinitely easier. But we've spent too long marveling. The time has arrived to consider the consequences of these monopolies, to reassert our own role in determining the human path. Once we cross certain thresholds—once we transform the values of institutions, once we abandon privacy—there's no turning back, no restoring our lost individuality.

OVER THE GENERATIONS, we've been through revolutions like this before. Back so many years ago, we delighted in the wonders of television dinners and the other newfangled foods that suddenly filled our kitchens: plastic-encased slices of cheese, oozing pizzas that emerged from a crust of ice, bags of crunchy tater tots. In the history of man, these seemed breakthrough innovations. Time-consuming tasks—shopping for ingredients; each of those tedious steps in a recipe, with their trail of collaterally crusted pots and pans—were suddenly and miraculously consigned to history.

The revolution in cuisine wasn't just enthralling. It was transformational. New products embedded themselves deeply in everyday life, so much so that it took decades for us to understand the price we paid for their convenience, efficiency, and abundance. These foods were feats of engineering all right—but they were engineered to make us fat. Their delectable taste required massive quantities of sodium and sizable stockpiles of lipids, which happened to reset our pallets and made it harder to sate hunger. It took vast new quantities of meat and corn to fabricate these dishes, a spike in demand that re-created the very essence of American agriculture and exacted a terrible environmental toll. A whole new system of industrial farming emerged, with penny-conscious conglomerates cramming chickens into feces-covered pens and stuffing them full of antibiotics. By the time we came to understand the consequences of our revised patterns of consumption, the damage had been done to our waistline, longevity, soul, and planet.

Something like the midcentury food revolution is now re-ordering the production and consumption of knowledge. Our intellectual habits are being scrambled by the dominant firms. Just as Nabisco and Kraft wanted to change how we eat and what we eat, Amazon, Facebook, and Google aspire to alter how we read and what we read. The biggest tech companies are, among other things, the most powerful gatekeepers the world has ever known. Google helps us sort the Internet by providing a sense of hierarchy to information; Facebook uses its algorithms and its intricate understanding of our social circles to sort the news we encounter; Amazon bestrides book publishing with its overwhelming hold on that market.

Such dominance endows these companies with the ability to remake the markets they control. As with the food giants, the big tech companies have given rise to a new science that aims to construct products that pander to the tastes of their consumers. They want to overhaul the entire chain of cultural production, so that they can capture greater profit. Intellectuals, freelance writers, investigative journalists, and midlist novelists are the analog to the family farmers, who have always struggled but simply can't compete in this transformed economy.

In the realm of knowledge, monopoly and conformism are inseparable perils. Monopoly is the danger that a powerful firm will use its dominance to squash the diversity of competition. Conformism is the danger that one of those monopolistic firms, intentionally or inadvertently, will use its dominance to squash diversity of opinion and taste. Concentration is followed by homogenization. With food, we only belatedly understood this pattern.

I WASN'T ALWAYS SO SKEPTICAL. At my first job, I would eat lunch staring at the Berlin Wall, its impressive thickness, all of its divots and bruises. The wall had defined the impenetrable boundary of an empire; now it casually decorated a new center of power in the world. This section of the wall belonged to Bill Gates and it resided in Microsoft's cafeteria.

My career in journalism began at Gates's software company. Microsoft had just built a new campus—centered on a quad, with a stream running through it—in the suburbs of Seattle to house all of its newly launched media. The company had created a women's magazine called *Underwire* (wonder why that one failed), an automotive magazine, and other sites devoted to urban life. After graduating from college, I flew west to be the low person on the masthead at a new outlet called *Slate*, which would become Microsoft's higher-brow, general interest offering.

These early efforts at Internet journalism were exhilarating. Our readers absorbed us on screens, which suggested a need for different styles of writing. But of what sort? We were no longer constrained by the mail and the printing press, so how often would we publish? Daily? Hourly? All of the conventions of writing felt thrillingly up for grabs.

As with so many aspects of the Internet, Microsoft had misjudged the shape of things to come. Microsoft tried to refashion itself as a state-of-the art media company, but its efforts were clunky and expensive. It made the mistake of actually producing editorial content. Its successors—Facebook, Google, Apple—didn't repeat that error. They surpassed Microsoft by adapting a revolutionary approach: the domination of media without hiring writers and editors, without owning much of anything.

Over the decades, the Internet revolutionized reading patterns. Instead of beginning with the home pages for *Slate* or the *New York Times*, a growing swath of readers now encounters articles through Google, Facebook, Twitter, and Apple. Sixty-two percent of Americans get their news through social media, and most of it via Facebook; a third of all traffic to media sites flows from Google. This has placed media in a state of abject financial dependence on tech companies. To survive, media companies lost track of their values. Even journalists of the highest integrity have internalized a new mind-set; they worry about how to successfully pander to Google's and Facebook's algorithms. In pursuit of clicks, some of our nation's most important purveyors of news have embraced sensationalism; they have published dubious stories; they have heaped attention on propagandists and conspiracists, one of whom was elected president of the United States. Facebook and Google have created a world where the old boundaries between fact and falsehood have eroded, where misinformation spreads virally.

I experienced an industrial-strength version of this narrative. Most of my career was spent at the *New Republic*—a little magazine based in Washington, always with fewer than one hundred thousand subscribers, devoted to politics and literature. We sputtered our way through the convulsions of the Internet era, until Chris Hughes bought the magazine in 2012. Chris wasn't just a savior; he was a face of the zeitgeist. At Harvard, Chris had roomed with Mark Zuckerberg, who had anointed him one of the first employees of Facebook. Chris gave our fusty old magazine a millennial imprimatur, a bigger budget, and an insider's knowledge of social media. We felt as if we carried the hopes of journalism, which was yearning for a dignified solution to all that ailed it. Chris hired me to edit the *New Republic*—a position I had held once before—and we began to remake the magazine, setting out to fulfill our own impossibly high expectations.

In the end, those expectations were too much for us to sustain. We couldn't move quickly enough to suit Chris. Our traffic boomed, but not exponentially. We never sufficiently mastered social media, in his view. My relationship with Chris frayed disastrously. He fired me after two and a half years—a bust-up interpreted widely as a parable of Silicon Valley's failure to understand the journalistic world over which it now exerted so much influence. There's no doubt that this experience informs the argument of this book.

I hope this book doesn't come across as fueled by anger, but I don't want to deny my anger either. The tech companies are destroying something precious, which is the possibility of contemplation. They have created a world in which we're constantly watched and always distracted. Through their accumulation of data, they have constructed a portrait of our minds, which they use to invisibly guide mass behavior (and increasingly individual behavior) to further their financial interests. They have eroded the integrity of institutions—media, publishing—that supply the intellectual material that provokes thought and guides democracy. Their most precious asset is our most precious asset, our attention, and they have abused it.

The companies have already succeeded in their goal of altering human evolution. We've all become a bit cyborg. Our phone is an extension of our memory; we've outsourced basic mental functions to algorithms; we've handed over our secrets to be stored on servers and mined by computers. What we need to always remember is that we're not just merging with machines, but with the companies that run the machines. This book is about the ideas that fuel these companies—and the imperative of resisting them.

THE MONOPOLISTS OF MIND

One

THE VALLEY IS WHOLE, THE WORLD IS ONE

BEFORE THE RISE OF SILICON VALLEY, monopoly was a pejorative in the dictionary of American life. Of course, the dirty word was joyously pursued. Businesses always aggressively aspired to achieve a state of complete and total dominance over markets. Most modern economics textbooks would describe that ambition as healthy and normal. Still, monopoly was a culturally unacceptable and politically dangerous goal to blare. Except in a few isolated cases, the true forerunners of today's giants, that goal was hardly ever vocalized in Thomas Jefferson's native land, which romanticized competition as the best hedge against dangerous concentrations of power. Even as the American government stopped doing much to actively constrain monopoly in the 1980s, companies continued to respect the old tradition of paying homage to the virtues of rigorous competition.

Then along came the new giants of tech. Silicon Valley's biggest companies don't merely crave monopoly as a matter of profit;

its pundits and theorists don't merely tolerate gigantism as a fact of economic life. In the great office parks south of San Francisco, monopoly is a spiritual yearning, a concept unabashedly embraced. Big tech considers the concentration of power in its companies—in the networks they control—an urgent social good, the precursor to global harmony, a necessary condition for undoing the alienation of humankind.

At their most idealistic moments, the tech giants drape their pursuit of monopoly in grandiose rhetoric about human rights and connection—a lofty sense of self-mission that makes the growth of these networks an imperative; their size becomes an end unto itself. They aspire to escape competition, to exist on their own plane, so they can fulfill their transcendent potential. Their dangerous dream has such a firm footing because it has such a long pedigree. Silicon Valley's craving for monopoly stretches back, strangely enough, to the counterculture of the 1960s, where it emerged from the most lyrical of visions of peace and love. More specifically, it begins with a crown prince of hippiedom.

STEWART BRAND WOULD DRIVE his truck down the San Francisco Midpeninsula, through the dissipating fog of the early sixties. The sticker on his bumper protested, "Custer Died for Your Sins." On his exposed chest rested a string of beads. Citizens of the acid scene, of which Brand was a leading light, thought of him as an "Indian freak." It was a romance that first stirred when a family friend asked Brand to photograph the Warm Springs Reservation for a brochure, and that culminated in his marriage to Lois Jennings, an Ottawa. To Brand, the child of an advertising executive, Native Americans were a revelation. His father had written a script for the conformist consumerism of the fifties, and Native Americans were the living, breathing refutation of it.

Like so many white men before him, Brand found authenticity on the reservation that felt painfully absent in his own life. The reservation was a refuge, a bastion that stubbornly refused to partake in planetary destruction and clung to a "cosmic consciousness." In an especially groovy mood, Brand once quipped, "[Indians] are so planetary they also tend to be extra-planetary." To spread the values that he first found in Warm Springs, Brand created a small troupe of dancers that performed a multimedia show he called "America Needs Indians." Replete with flashing lights, music, and projected images, the show was "a peyote meeting without peyote," in Brand's telling.

This spectacle was an early glimpse of Brand's career as an impresario—one who would shape the future of technology. His gift was to channel the spiritual longings of his generation, and then to explain how they could be fulfilled by technology. He made his case in books and articles, but those were his relatively square undertakings. He created a new genre of publication that, more or less, hyperlinked to the texts of his fellow travelers. Long before TED, he created a chin-tugging conference circuit.

Brand would come to inspire a revolution in computing. Engineers across Silicon Valley revered Brand for explaining the profound potential of their work in ways they couldn't always see or articulate. Brand gathered a devoted following because he brought to technology a rousing sense of idealism. Where politics failed to transform humanity, computers just might.

That dream of transformation—a world healed by technology, brought together into a peaceful model of collaboration—

carries a charming innocence. In Silicon Valley, this naive belief has been handed down through ages. Even the most hard-nosed corporations have internalized it. What began as a stirring dream—humanity tied together into a single transcendent network—has become the basis for monopoly. In the hands of Facebook and Google, Brand's vision is a pretext for domination.

BEFORE STEWART BRAND COULD REMAKE technology, he needed to mold the sixties. It is a story that begins, as many tales of the prehippie years do, a bit aimlessly. After boarding at Exeter and graduating from Stanford, Brand enlisted in the army. His experience in the barracks ended unhappily, but it also supplied him with a measure of organizational acumen and managerial chops. These skills never did fail him, even after he placed tabs of LSD on his tongue. (He began messing around with acid in 1962, when it could be procured from legitimate medical experimenters.) Brand was the master of the uptight, straitlaced tasks that flummoxed most of his long-haired friends—renting a hall, publicizing an event. When he linked up with the writer Ken Kesey and his storied posse of drug-dabbling Merry Pranksters, he represented the "restrained, reflective wing" of that Day-Glo band of hipsters, at least in *The Electric Kool-Aid Acid Test*, Tom Wolfe's travelogue through the emerging counterculture. Though Brand wore a top hat with a flower, and he spoke in impish aphorisms, he remained a neatnik with a filing cabinet.

His pièce de résistance was organizing the Trips Festival, the greatest of the Acid Test parties that Kesey's crew hosted in San Francisco to celebrate their favorite drug. Brand put together a program for three days of psychedelia, which helped launch the 1960s, as we now know them. Among other things, the extravaganza introduced the Grateful Dead to the world; it gathered six thousand hippies and gave them a sense of belonging to a culture, or rather a counterculture. Brand placed his obsessions center stage on the first night of the festival, giving the America Needs Indians troupe prime billing.

All the lights and images that Brand deployed were like LSD, an attempt to artificially induce a heightened sense of consciousness. America needed Indians, and it needed acid, too. A jolt to rouse the country from its gray flannel numbness. In time, Brand would ascribe the same mind-bending powers to computers. But before he celebrated those machines, he didn't much like them. Everything the nascent counterculture would come to despise—the mindless submission of the herd, the tyranny of bureaucracy—could be reduced to a pungent symbol, the computer. When Brand later looked back on the sixties, he recalled, "Most of our generation scorned computers as the embodiment of centralized control."

Across the bay in Berkeley, criticism of the computer could be heard in the earliest rumblings of the New Left. Mario Savio, the oratorical leader of the Free Speech Movement on campus, compared the oppressive forces at the university (and in society) to technology: "There's a time when the operation of the machine becomes so odious, makes you so sick at heart, that you can't take part. You can't even tacitly take part. And you've got to put your bodies upon the gears and upon the wheels." But the metaphor was often more specific. As Savio put it: "At Cal you're little more than an IBM card." Indeed, protesting students strung computer cards around their necks, with holes stamped through them to read STRIKE. They mockingly wrote, "Please do not fold, bend, spindle or mutilate me."

This critique was more than fair. To begin, there was IBM, the opaque corporation that manufactured the machines. By the late 1950s, IBM controlled 70 percent of the domestic computer market, with no true competitor trailing it. This monopoly was a product of savvy engineering, but also of the full support of the Pentagon and other branches of the state. (These subsidies helped the United States overtake first-rate European engineers, who enjoyed no such state support.) IBM named one of its first models, the 701, the "Defense Calculator," to pander to its primary market. Nearly all of the 701s it manufactured were rented to either the Defense Department or aerospace companies. A few years later, the NSA subsidized the development of a new model, a collaboration called "STRETCH," so long as the machines could be calibrated to suit the agencies' distinct needs. Paul Ceruzzi, a careful, nonideological historian of technology, has bracingly described the era: "U.S. computing from 1945 through the 1970s was dominated by large, centralized systems under tight controls, and these were not at odds with the Soviet political system."

The machines, in fact, looked perfectly malevolent. Until the 1970s, most computers were massive, immovable blocks, like the behemoth institutions that used them. Whole rooms were required to house these early models. Because these instruments were so expensive and delicate, they were guarded vigilantly. To submit data, suppliants approached a window and handed punch cards to white-coated, skinny-tied technicians, a group invariably described as a "priesthood." These punch cards resembled nothing so much as a multiple-choice form, that essential instrument of bureaucracy. This clinical approach suited the postwar elite, with its technocratic bent and obsession with efficiency.

Stewart Brand believed many of the worst things that one could say about computers. And yet, he held out hope that they might remake the world for the better. In part, the flicker of optimism was generational. Baby boomers grew up in a world steeped in technology—rock and roll, automobiles, television. They enjoyed modernity far too much to mount a full-throated counteroffensive. As Theodore Roszak, the New Left theorist, later explained: "Side by side with the appeal of folk music and primitive ways, handicrafts and organic husbandry, there was a childlike, Oh Wow! confabulation with the spaceships and miraculous mechanisms that would make Stanley Kubrick's *2001* and the television series *Star Trek* cult favorites."

Brand's own prophecy about technology came in a series of epiphanies, only one of which was induced by drugs. Sitting atop his apartment building in the hipster enclave of North Beach, he covered himself in a blanket. A string of thoughts passed through his mind. *Why weren't the buildings in front of him arrayed in perfectly parallel lines? Damn, must be the curvature of the Earth. Definitely, the curvature of the Earth. Hmmmm, you know, with all those satellites staring down on the planet, why isn't there a photograph of the Earth? Not just a photograph, but a color photograph. Not just the Earth, but the WHOLE Earth. If there were a picture of the whole Earth, man, that would change everything.* Thus began Brand's campaign of heckling NASA into releasing a color photograph of the whole Earth. He soon hitchhiked east to sell buttons on college campuses, which trumpeted his demand. This crusade, quixotic as it now sounds, helped awaken the environmental movement.

A second epiphany built on the first. Returning from his father's funeral, he pondered how he might spend the chunk of money he had just inherited. He began to think about all his friends who had decamped to communes. It was easy to see why the communes grabbed hold of his imagination. Starting with the Summer of Love in 1967 and continuing through the *annus horribilis* of 1968, hundreds of thousands of young Americans, driven by hope and fear, went to live off the grid in self-sufficient collective communities. They sprouted villages with names like Drop City and Twin Oaks, in places like the New Mexico desert, the Tennessee mountains, and the Northern California forests. (By one estimate, the commune population swelled to 750,000 in the early seventies.) Sitting on the plane, Brand had the notion that he might drive a truck to these settlements to sell tools and other goods that would help the communards thrive. "This was a way to be of use to communes without actually having to live on one," he would later joke.

His truck never quite took off, but the core concept morphed into something much bigger and more resonant. He created the *Whole Earth Catalog*, which was really more like an entirely new literary genre—or what Steve Jobs called "one of the bibles of my generation." During its four years of existence, the *Whole Earth Catalog* sold 2.5 million copies and won a National Book Award. The subtitle of the catalog was "access to tools." There were plenty described in its pages, though it didn't actually sell any, except from a storefront that Brand operated in the heart of what would become Silicon Valley. The catalog pointed readers toward calculators and jackets and geodesic domes, as well as books and magazines. The goods themselves were less important than the catalog's theoretical arguments about them. In an early issue, it announced:

> We are as gods and might as well get good at it. So far, re-motely done power and glory—as via government, big busi-ness, formal education, church—has succeeded to the point where gross defects obscure actual gains. In response to this dilemma and to these gains a realm of intimate, personal power is developing—power of the individual to conduct his own education, find his own inspiration, shape his own envir-onment, and share his adventure with whoever is interested. Tools that aid this process are sought and promoted by the WHOLE EARTH CATALOG.

Brand's manifesto distilled the thinking of the commune movement and then advanced it in crucial ways. Technology, he argued, had created the ills of the world. Only technology could solve them. Tools, liberated from the hands of the monopolists and militarists, could empower individuals to become more self-sufficient and more self-expressive. Power Tools to the People, you could say. If some of these sentiments sound familiar, it is because they have echoed in dozens of Apple commercials over the years.

In a way, this was a theory of radical individualism and self-reliance—a forerunner of Silicon Valley libertarianism. But Brand had studied the works of such thinkers as Buckminster Fuller, Norbert Wiener, and Marshall McLuhan. All of his intel-lectual heroes wrote about the importance of looking at systems and networks. This was where the notion of the Whole Earth came in. Brand wanted his readers to think ecologically, to see how everything relates to everything else, to understand their place in the web of life. As the back cover of the catalog phrased it, "We can't put it together. It is together."

The *Whole Earth Catalog* is a foundational text of Silicon Valley—which helps account for the culture of the place. Despite the venture capitalists and the Teslas, Silicon Valley remains infused with the trace residue of the commune. It's the reason that CEOs sit in the middle of open offices that ostensibly eschew organizational hierarchy, wearing the same T-shirt as the lumpenprogrammer across the room. And even though Silicon Valley's monopolies exist for the sake of profit, they view themselves as revolutionary agents, elevating the world to the state of oneness that Brand spent his life chasing. As Fred Turner has written in his important book *From Counterculture to Cyberculture*, "[The catalog] helped create the conditions under which microcomputers and computer networks could be imagined as tools of liberation."

WHEN JOBS DESCRIBED THE *Whole Earth Catalog* as a "bible" to his generation, he really meant to his generation of techies and hackers, the vanguard of geeks that revolutionized computing. All the rudiments of personal computing were, more or less, developed by the late sixties. Thanks to DEC, the Massachusetts hardware company, there were new examples of massive mainframes shrunk to more approachable microprocessors. Designers at Stanford had created the mouse. The Defense Department had wired the first internet. Visionary technologists like Doug Engelbart (inventor of the mouse) had imagined a future where machines played a much more intimate role in the lives of everyday people. But they spoke in jargon—and the machines were still too expensive, too large, and too confusing to be placed on office desks, let alone into homes.

Innovations don't magically appear or simply proceed on the basis of some scientific logic; the culture prods them into existence. The notion of personalized computing had yet to cohere. It was arguably Brand who crystallized the ideas that would inspire the engineers to make that leap. The *Whole Earth Catalog* transposed the values of the counterculture into technology. And over time, he began to show how the computer—that monstrous invention of big institutions—could be harnessed as a tool for personal liberation and communal connection.

It is an important fact of technological history that the outskirts of San Francisco were the national epicenter of both psychedelics and computing. Because of that geographical confluence, young engineers were unusually open to Stewart Brand's message. That was especially true at Xerox's famed freewheeling cauldron of creativity, its Palo Alto Research Center (PARC). One of the chief engineers there, Alan Kay, ordered every book listed in the *Whole Earth Catalog* and assembled them in an office library. Over the years, Kay would lavishly credit Brand for pointing toward the future: "For us at PARC, he was the guy who was giving us the early warning system about what computers were going to be."

Having absorbed Brand into their work, the PARC engineers let him hang out in their lab. He would describe what he saw in a seminal article that he wrote for *Rolling Stone* in 1972. The article was a vivid, energetic piece of New Journalism: "The most bzz-bzz-busy scene I've been around since Merry Prankster Acid

Tests." Brand depicted the computer scientists exactly as he wanted to see them—as the great emancipators of technology: "Those magnificent men with their flying machines, scouting a leading edge of technology which has an odd softness to it; outlaw country, where rules are not decree or routine so much as the starker demands of what's possible." The engineers had indeed begun to develop machines that were a decade ahead of their time, and too radical for the corporate suits at Xerox to fully comprehend. Their most legendary prototype was a computer with many of the elements that would later appear in the Macintosh—no coincidence, because Steve Jobs was enraptured by the innovations he witnessed in a highly mythologized visit to PARC in the winter of 1979.

But what made Brand's article so influential is that he took the impulses of the engineers and translated them into pithy phrases—and these pithy phrases, in turn, gave direction to the work of the engineers. Brand painted a glorious image of computing. What the communes failed to accomplish, the computers would complete. "When computers become available to everybody, the hackers take over: We are all Computer Bums, all more empowered as individuals and as co-operators. That might enhance things . . . like the richness and rigor of spontaneous creation and of human interaction . . . of sentient interaction." Two years later, when he grew this article into a book, he injected an important new phrase into the lexicon: "the personal computer."

IT DOESN'T BODE WELL for the world that the lineage of the tech companies stretches back to the communes. That experiment ended in shambles—the communities dissolved into cults of personality, small villages riven by rivalries. All the gorgeous visions of democracy and collectivism culminated in authoritarianism and crushing disappointment. In 1971, Stewart Brand pulled the plug on the *Whole Earth Catalog* after four years of publication. To honor the retirement of his zeitgeist-bending creation, he threw a "Demise Party." A thousand catalog devotees journeyed to the extravaganza, another of his performance pieces. He gathered his hippie friends in the Palace of Fine Arts, an imposing old-world edifice down by the San Francisco Marina. Brand strode through the event wearing a black cassock, a tuned-in Grim Reaper.

Even a rugged optimist such as Brand found it hard to push away dark thoughts at this nadir. His marriage collapsed. Thoughts of suicide would linger in his head. But his faith in technology remained undimmed. Brand hadn't cared that deeply about politics and hadn't spent much time pondering the nature of capitalism. His concerns were far more spiritual. What he still craved was the sensation of wholeness—the profound belonging and authenticity he associated with the reservations and communes. They didn't harbor a shred of alienation. They were at one with humanity. It was the same craving he felt when contemplating that missing photograph of Earth. This thinking was the exact opposite of Ayn Rand's vision of libertarianism; a hunger for cooperation, sharing, and a self-conscious awareness of our place in a larger system. Brand could express this sentiment only in gusts of rhetoric that would never survive rigorous analysis, except for the force with which they were exhaled: "Ever since there were two organisms, life has been a matter of coevolution, life growing ever more richly on life. . . . We can ask what kinds of dependency we prefer, but that's our only choice."

However eloquently expressed, such thoughts weren't entirely original. Brand borrowed heavily from others, especially Marshall McLuhan, the Canadian academic turned pop icon. Unlike his stuffy colleagues, McLuhan engaged with the culture as it was lived in the sixties—not the work of modernist novelists and action painters, but television, radio, and movies. He was lithe and gnomic, a strangely appealing fixture on TV talk shows, not to mention a perfectly deadpan actor in Woody Allen's *Annie Hall*. It was often hard to tell what he actually believed, given his penchant for explaining himself in seemingly profound, and profoundly opaque, paradoxes. ("I don't necessarily agree with everything I say," he once admitted.) But even his muddiest prophecies could easily be mined for zippy, quotable formulations.

McLuhan claimed to make no moral judgments about the impending future he described, yet his passages about new technologies were often tinged by euphoria. In his books, McLuhan had predicted that new technologies could, if handled judiciously, tie the world together into a network: "Today, after more than a century of electric technology, we have extended our central nervous system itself in a global embrace, abolishing both space and time as far as our planet is concerned."

McLuhan hinted that this network had the potential to wrap like a magical bandage around the world, closing its wounds without any trace of a scar. The fragmentation of humanity was an understandable concern for a generation born in the shadow of a total war and living under the constant threat of a nuclear conflagration. There was a more personal form of fragmentation that plagued postwar America, too—a sense that all the paper-pushing and file cabinets had divided workers from their creativity, rendering them miserable, isolated automatons. But that plague of alienation, McLuhan suggested, was hardly implacable.

The healing powers of the network could be found in McLuhan's famous maxim: *The medium is the message*. Technology was the thing that mattered. He heaped blame upon Gutenberg's invention, print, a medium he believed divided the world, isolating us from our fellow humans in the antisocial act of reading. "The alphabet is a technology of visual fragmentation and specialization," he lamented. It produced a "desert of classified data." His critique was actually a lament—he longed for the world before print, for oral culture, with its face-to-face interactions. The perfect technology would revive the spirit of that bygone culture, but on a planetary scale, transforming the world into one big, happy tribe. Or, it would become a "global village," to use his other cliché-destined phrase—and the warmth of that village would counteract destructive individualism and all the other fragmentary forces in the world.

Most promising of all the new technologies was the computer. It is true, McLuhan saw potential downsides to the invention and to the global village he described—rumors might travel fast, privacy might not survive all the new opportunities for surveillance. Still, his descriptions of the computer echoed Brand's. McLuhan also passionately craved wholeness and then some, which he described rhapsodically:

> Today computers hold out the promise of a means of instant translation of any code or language into any other code or language. The computer, in short, promises by technology a Pentecostal condition of universal understanding and unity. The next logical step would seem to be, not to translate, but to bypass languages in favor of a general cosmic consciousness which might be very like the collective unconscious

dreamt of by [twentieth-century French philosopher Henri] Bergson. The condition of "weightlessness," that biologists say promises a physical immortality, may be paralleled by the condition of speechlessness that could confer a perpetuity of collective harmony and peace.

Eternal life, eternal peace . . . the devoutly Catholic McLuhan had ventured beyond political prophecy to a more biblical form.

EVERY SIGNIFICANT technological development since has come wrapped in McLuhan's aspiration: the desire for machines to usher in a new era of cooperation. That's what J.C.R. Licklider meant when he explained how his invention of the Internet would erase social isolation: "Life will be happier for the on-line individual." And how Tim Berners-Lee described the possibilities of the World Wide Web he created: "Hope in life comes from the interconnections among all the people in the world." The dream of stitching the world into a global village has been embodied in the nomenclature of modern technology—the net is interconnected, the Web is worldwide, media is social. And the dream has fueled a succession of grand collaborative projects, cathedrals of knowledge built without any intention of profiting from the creation, from the virtual communities of the nineties to Linux to Wikipedia to the Creative Commons. It's found in the very idea of open-source software. Such notions of sharing were once idealistic gestures and the reveries of shaggy inventors, but they have become so much the norm that they have been embraced by capitalism. The business plans of the most spectacularly successful firms in history, Google and Facebook, are all about wiring the world into one big network—a network where individuals work together, in a spirit of altruism, to share information.

There is a theory of knowledge embedded in this celebration of sharing: the notion that individuals can achieve only a limited understanding of the world while reading and thinking at their own desks. Before the arrival of the new technologies, information, like the isolated scholar, was atomized. But now, information can be sorted and processed by a much larger community—that could correct mistakes, add insights, and revise conclusions. Technology enabled what H. G. Wells once called the World Brain, or what *Wired* editor Kevin Kelly called the hive mind.

The assumption that undergirds this strain of technological thinking is that humans aren't simply self-interested economic creatures. Linus Torvalds, the engineer who created Linux, argued, "Money is not the greatest of motivators. It's been well established that folks do their best work when they are driven by a passion." At times, this collectivist view of human nature was difficult to discern. The representative figure of early computing was the hacker—a radical individualist, who liked to thumb his nose at big institutions. Hackers were portrayed as loners, glued to their seats and screens; they were geniuses who depended on nothing more than their self-taught acumen. (One prominent metaphor depicted the early inhabitants of cyberspace as pioneers on an electronic frontier, bravely setting forth on their own.) But in the end, the hackers were misunderstood figures. They wanted nothing more than to belong, to subsume their brilliant selves in an even more incandescent whole, to lose themselves in the poetry of community.

BUT THERE WAS TENSION in the dream. Contradictions that wouldn't easily melt away. On the one hand, the technologists aspired to create a world liberated from the control of mega-institutions. The old hatred for the likes of IBM never did fade. On the other hand, they created networks that were designed to be all-encompassing and unrivaled. There can be only one global village. These structures were the greatest business opportunities ever imagined—and only the innocence of faith could blind one to the possibility that they would fall into the hands of big firms. In the end, the technologists' disdain for authority was really just a stance, an emotionally gratifying one, and it wasn't the meat of the vision. The more important thing was the wholeness.

That is the reason that the history of computing follows such a predictable pattern. Each pathbreaking innovation promises to liberate technology from the talons of the monopolists, to create a new network so democratic that it will transform human nature. Somehow, in each instance, humanity remains its familiar self. Instead of profound redistributions of power, the new networks are captured by new monopolies, each more powerful and sophisticated than the one before it. The personal computer came to be dominated by a single innovation-inhibiting firm (Microsoft). Access to the Internet soon required handing over substantial monthly sums to telecommunication toll collectors who carved up the map into zones of barely challenged supremacy (Comcast, Verizon, Time Warner). Meanwhile, one site (Google) emerged as the portal to knowledge; another (Amazon) as the starting point of all commerce. And even though we can talk about social networks in the plural, really only one (Facebook) encompasses nearly two billion individuals.

There's always been a strange, unacknowledged convergence in the thinking of technological dreamers and the rapacious industrial monopolists of the Gilded Age. Both like to imagine escaping the rigors of competitive capitalism; both wax elegiac about the virtues of "cooperation," which they invoke as a matter of economic necessity. There are certain systems—the telephone and telegraph are classic examples—that simply never would have flourished in a competitive market. The costs of setting up a massive network are immense. Imagine the expense of laying down all those lines crisscrossing the continent. The inefficiency of rival networks is too great. We must, therefore, forgive the size of the firms that provide these essential services—and give them space to cooperate with the government and other big firms so that they can prudently eliminate waste and make disinterested strategic choices. This was what the visionary Theodore Vail, who built AT&T in the first decades of the last century, claimed: "Competition means strife, industrial warfare; it means contention; it oftentimes means taking advantage of or resorting to any means that the conscience of the contestants . . . will permit." Even the railroad barons, the most conniving creatures that capitalism ever created, extolled the virtues of altruistic collaboration. J. P. Morgan himself sincerely believed this gospel. As the biographer Ron Chernow writes, "America's most famous financier was a sworn foe of free markets."

Such arguments are increasingly familiar in Silicon Valley. It's the premise of a whole shelf of books on strategy. (Sample title: *Modern Monopolies: What It Takes to Dominate the 21st Century*

Economy.) The most important prophet of the new monopoly is an investor named Peter Thiel. He isn't just any investor. His successes include PayPal, Facebook, Palantir, and SpaceX, an almost unrivaled record of sniffing out winners before they become chic, which suggests a deeper understanding of technology and its trajectory. Thiel can be a wildly idiosyncratic thinker, which has justly earned him opprobrium in recent years. During the 2016 presidential campaign, he supported Donald Trump. He also quietly bankrolled retired wrestler Hulk Hogan's lawsuit against a gossip site. All these pernicious extracurricular activities distract from his core strength: He's a more rigorous thinker than the others in his field. Though he mouths many of the libertarian clichés of his social set, he has a talent for explaining his underlying assumptions. Thiel abhors the values of Darwinian competition. Indeed, he dismisses competition as a "relic of history." In a short treatise called *Zero to One*, he wrote, "More than anything else, competition is an ideology—*the* ideology—that pervades our society and distorts our thinking. We preach competition, internalize its necessity, and enact its commandments; and as a result, we trap ourselves within it—even though the more we compete, the less we gain." By idolizing competition, we fail to appreciate the values of monopolies. Without having to worry about rivals, monopolies can focus on important things— they can treat their workers well, they can focus on solving important problems and generating world-changing innovation. They can "transcend the daily brute struggle for survival."

It's pretty clear that most of his colleagues in Silicon Valley agree that monopoly is the natural, desirable order of things. That's why start-up companies no longer dream of displacing Google or Facebook, but launch themselves with the ultimate aspiration of getting bought by the giants. (On its shopping expeditions over the years, Google has acquired two hundred companies.) In the tech industry, fierce corporate rivalry is regarded as an impossibility, and anathema to the very essence of the network. For the most part, the tech giants respect an *entente cordiale* among themselves. Apple, for instance, used to insist that its rivals never poach from its ranks of employees. The coziness can be gleaned from the balance sheets: Google pays $1 billion each year so that Apple will use its search engine. While he was Google CEO, Eric Schmidt also served on Apple's board. Like nineteenth-century European powers, each company does little to impinge on the other's sphere of influence, competing only on the fringes of empire. Marc Andreessen, one of the Valley's most venerable characters, is blunt about this tendency toward monopoly: "The big technology markets actually tend to be winner take all. There is this presumption—in normal markets you can have Pepsi and Coke. In technology markets in the long run you tend to only have one, or rather the number one company." That is the nub of it: In Silicon Valley, everything is one; it's always been one.

Two

THE GOOGLE THEORY
OF HISTORY

THE NETWORK WANTS ITS TENDRILS to cradle the world, wrapping itself around everyone and everything. In the summer of 2015, Google renamed itself Alphabet, which was a statement about the company's place in history. A search engine called Google remained, but the company had become so much more than that. It is a commercial bazaar, a backbone of Internet infrastructure, a software company, a hardware company, a phone company, an advertising agency, a home appliance company, a life sciences company, a machine learning company, an automobile company, a social media company, and a TV network. One of its subsidiaries claims to counter political extremism; another launches balloons to transmit the Internet to far corners of the globe. The alphabet was one of humanity's greatest innovations, the sort of everlasting achievement that the company intends to foment again and again.

Bluster pours forth from the tech elite, and much of the

world tends to look at their lengthy inventory of grandiose projects as vanity. If Jeff Bezos wants to launch rockets into space, then Elon Musk will do him one better and colonize Mars. But Silicon Valley is hardly distinguished by the hegemonic egos of its leaders, especially relative to finance or media. What makes Big Tech different is that it pursues these projects with a theological sense of conviction—which makes its efforts both wondrous and dangerous.

At the epicenter of Google's bulging portfolio is one master project: The company wants to create machines that replicate the human brain, and then advance beyond. This is the essence of its attempts to build an unabridged database of global knowledge and its efforts to train algorithms to become adept at finding patterns, teaching them to discern images and understand language. Taking on this grandiose assignment, Google stands to transform life on the planet, precisely as it boasted it would. The laws of man are a mere nuisance that can only slow down such work. Institutions and traditions are rusty scrap for the heap. The company rushes forward, with little regard for what it tramples, on its way toward the New Jerusalem.

LARRY PAGE'S FAITH in this mission was his patrimony. His dad wasn't like the others. His appearance was different, that was for sure. Polio, contracted on a childhood vacation to Tennessee, had stunted the growth of one leg. His gait was uneven; at times, he struggled to breathe. When he felt good, Carl Page, Sr., was a bundle of magical enthusiasms. He would scurry down the corridors of the computer science department, summoning colleagues to his office to announce one of his many big ideas. He could be an enchanted seer. In the eighties, years before Tim Berners-Lee's invention of the Web, he would riff about the potential of hyperlinks. The students at Michigan State found Carl's passions to be both inspiring and a bit overwhelming. His faith in their skills occasionally would stretch beyond the reality of their expertise. There was the time, for instance, he assigned kids to write code that would enable a robot to plug itself into electrical outlets.

Carl Page focused pedagogic attention on Larry and his older brother, Carl Jr. He wanted them to grow up in the future, a place where his own mind tended to reside. Under his supervision, the family's ranch house in the Pine Crest section of East Lansing was, by the eight-track standards of the era, transformed into an electronic wonderland.

When Larry was six, his dad brought home an Exidy Sorcerer computer—a cult favorite of European programmers—a machine so exotic that Carl Jr. had to compose its operating system from scratch. "I think I was the first kid in my elementary school to turn in a word-processed document," Larry would later recount. The house was strewn with copies of *Popular Science*, their Technicolor covers like movie posters, with images of robot-armed submarines and stealth jets. The magazine's celebration of tinkering perfectly expressed the spirit of the household, and all that inventiveness filtered down to the youngest son. Larry once gathered power tools from all corners of the house so that he could disassemble them and examine their innards. Even if this activity didn't have official parental sanction—and even if he didn't quite put things back together—Larry escaped reprimand. Mischief in the quest for technological knowledge was no vice. By the time he left for college in 1991, he had amassed sufficient prowess to convert Legos into an ink-jet printer.

If computers were rare in the Midwest of the late seventies, computer scientists were downright alien. Page's parents had migrated westward from their spiritual home in Ann Arbor, where they had earned their degrees, but not far enough. Carl took a job at Michigan State, which was hardly Stanford. He would help build a computing outpost on a periphery of the digital world. East Lansing didn't quite swing like the San Francisco Mid-peninsula, either. Carl stood somewhat apart from his Ward-and-June neighbors. His politics tilted a bit further left. He inherited those from his father, a line worker at the Chevrolet plant in Flint who carried a homemade iron bludgeon to stave off goons during the long strike of 1936–37. Carl even managed a hint of California groovy in his new environs. He would take Larry to Grateful Dead concerts.

Unconventionality wasn't just a personal style; it was a career necessity. Carl had chosen to pursue an audacious new specialty, a branch of computer science devoted to building machines that could simulate human thought. This subgenre of science fiction turned academic discipline goes by the name artificial intelligence (AI).

It was easy to see why this field would appeal to someone with Carl's streak of intellectual adventurousness. Yes, the pursuit of artificial intelligence required computational acumen and a knack for algorithmic thinking. But if you wanted to replicate the working of the human brain, you had to intimately understand your model. AI, in other words, required psychology. The engineers read Freud, just like the literary critics—and reinterpreted him for their own purposes. They debated Chomsky about the nature of the mind.

The AI pioneers formulated their own intoxicating theory of

the human mind. They believed that the brain is itself a computer—a device controlled by programs. This metaphor provided a fairly neat description of their own task: They were building a mechanical machine to imitate an organic one. But the human mind is a mysterious thing. So creating algorithms that replicate the inner workings of such an inscrutable mass of tissue was a complicated and controversial task. Carl Page had his own idea about how to go about it. He posited that procedures contained in *Robert's Rules of Order*, a late-nineteenth-century manual for running effective meetings, could provide the basis for building AI.

There weren't very many scientists working on artificial intelligence in those years. They made for a fascinating little subculture. That's how the sociologist Sherry Turkle studied them in her classic tome, *The Second Self*. Because she was perched at MIT herself, she had a fairly unimpeded view of her subjects. The portrait she constructed was so piercingly apt that they may not have been able to recognize themselves in it. Artificial intelligence, she concluded, wasn't just a lofty engineering goal; it was an ideology. She compared AI, with its theory about the programmable mind, to psychoanalysis and Marxism—as "a new way of understanding almost everything."

> In each case a central concept restructures understanding on a large scale: for the Freudian, the unconscious; for the Marxist, the relationship to the means of production. . . . [F]or the AI researcher, the idea of program has a transcendent value: it is taken as the key, the until now missing term for unlocking intellectual mysteries.

Carl Page was a rationalist. Yet some biographical accounts of Larry's childhood note that his father had instructed him with religious intensity. Over the dinner table, Carl would share the good news about AI that was arriving from the booming laboratories on the coasts. This wasn't simply a matter of filling conversation. It was instruction. His curriculum included field trips to various AI confabs. When the organizers of the International Joint Conference on Artificial Intelligence wouldn't allow Larry, a sixteen-year-old, into their convention hall, Carl broke from his jovial form and reamed the obstructionists.

It is a testament to Carl Page's teaching that his son went on to found the most successful, most ambitious AI company in history. Although we don't think of Google that way, AI is precisely the source of the company's greatness. Google uses algorithms, trained to think just like you. To accomplish this daunting task, Google must understand the intentions behind your query: When you typed "rock," did you mean the geological feature or the musical genre or the wrestler-turned-actor? Google's AI is so proficient that it can even supply the results for your query before you've finished typing it.

But, an heir to the great tradition of AI, Larry Page considers this accomplishment an insignificant step on the route to a much more profound mission—a mission in both the scientific and religious senses of the word. He has built his company so that it can achieve what is called "AI complete," the creation of machines with the ability to equal and eventually exceed human intelligence. A few years after he launched Google, he returned to give a talk at Stanford, where he and Sergey Brin had birthed their search engine. He told a group of students, "Well, I would say the mission I laid out for you will take us a little while since it's AI complete. It means its artificial intelligence. . . . If you solve search that means you can answer any question, which means you can do basically anything." The audacity of this claim made the audience laugh, a bit uncomfortably. But their discomfort only stirred Page to push forward with his point. "If we solve the problem I outlined, then we're doing everything."

In moments of candor, Page and Brin admit that they imagine going even further than that—it's not just about creating an artificial brain but welding it to the human. As Brin once told the journalist Steven Levy, "Certainly if you had all the world's information directly attached to your brain, or an artificial brain that was smarter than your brain, you'd be better off." Or as he added on a separate occasion, "Perhaps in the future, we can attach a little version of Google that you just plug into your brain."

Google may or may not ever achieve these grandiose goals, but that's how the company views its role. When Page describes Google reshaping the future of humanity, this isn't simply a description of the convenience it provides; what it aims to redirect is the course of evolution, in the Darwinian sense of the word. It's not too grandiose to claim that they are attempting to create a superior species, a species that transcends our natural form.

PAGE AND BRIN ARE CREATING a brain unhindered by human bias, uninfluenced by irrational desires and dubious sensory instructions that emanate from the body. In pursuing this goal, they are attempting to complete a mission that began long before the invention of the computer. Google is trying solve a problem that first emerged several centuries ago, amid the blazing battle between the entrenched church and the emerging science. It's a project that originated with modern philosophy itself and the figure of René Descartes.

A trace of Larry Page's vision could be spotted on a small ship on the North Sea in the early years of the seventeenth century. Belowdecks, Descartes slept. He often made such journeys. Over his life, he never quite settled. He could be proud and quarrelsome, doggedly private and deliberately enigmatic. Even with centuries of retrospect, we can't say what fueled his many unsettled years of travel, all the time he spent shuttling from one abode to the next like a fugitive.

Of his many destinations, Protestant Holland felt most like his home, an ease that was perhaps unexpected given his thoroughly Jesuit training. That's where he stayed longest and where he laid the tracks for his philosophy. Historians will note that it is, based on the evidence, also the locale where he lost his virginity to an Amsterdam housemaid. He recorded the fact of that event with scientific detachment on the flyleaf of a book, as if collecting results for an experiment. The daughter from that encounter was called Francine, and he had made plans for her study in France. But her life was crushingly short. She died of scarlet fever, not yet six.

Descartes enjoyed his sleep; profound revelations came to him in dreams. Entire mornings were often spent in bed. But that wasn't possible on this voyage. The ship's captain had been eyeing the philosopher with suspicion. He was especially keen to determine the contents of the trunk that sat beside Descartes's bed. In the middle of the night, he stormed the cabin and pried open the container. What he found inside was a startlingly life-like machine—a robot made of springs, an automaton. According to some reports, the machine closely resembled Francine, which was in fact what Descartes called it. Horrified by his discovery, the captain dragged Descartes's creation above deck and hurled it into the sea.

This story has been told and retold, especially by Descartes's detractors. It is certainly false, a manufactured smear. As one of his biographers points out, the tale carries a whiff of disturbing sexual innuendo. But his enemies contrived this fiction for a compelling reason: Descartes was indeed obsessed with automata, even if he didn't always keep one by his bed. During his life, the machine age was arriving in Europe, a subset of the great scientific revolution. In the gardens of the royal palaces, inventors unveiled incredible intricately engineered creations—hydraulically powered statues, figurines that played music, clockwork characters that whirled and gestured. Descartes daydreamed about building his own contraptions from springs and magnets. More important, automata were to play a central role in his effort to resolve the wars—between religions, between science and religion—tearing apart Europe.

The messy, war-torn seventeenth century touched Descartes directly. He served in both Catholic and Protestant armies in the Thirty Years War—an intramural fight over the religious future of Germany that ensnared the major European powers. Everything in Europe, during those years, seemed raw and unsettled. Despite Holland's relative tolerance, Descartes lived in mortal fear that the Inquisition might target him. To avoid Galileo's fate, he left manuscripts unpublished for years.

There's disagreement about the extent to which Descartes remained a devout Catholic, or a believer at all. (One could argue that his proofs of God's existence are so contorted that they must have been deliberately conceived to highlight the absurdity of his project.) However fervently he clung to his faith, his training and his travel had perfectly prepared him to broker a cease-fire in the conflict that pitted religion against science.

At the center of his theory were automata. The bodies of living creatures, even humans, were nothing more than machines. The human form—"an extended, non-thinking thing"—moved mindlessly in response to stimuli, as if it were composed of springs and levers. Our bodies could be described by scientific laws, just like the movement of the planets. If Descartes had stopped there, his theory would have infuriated the church. Catholic doctrine insisted that humans are the highest form of life, above all other beasts. But Descartes didn't stop there. He asserted that the human casing contains a divine instrument that elevates humankind above the animal kingdom. Inside our mortal hardware, the "prison of the body," as Descartes called it, resides the software of mind. In his theory, the mind was the place to find both the intellect and the immortal soul, the capacity for reason and man's most godlike qualities.

This was a gorgeous squaring of the circle. Descartes had somehow managed to use skepticism in service of orthodoxy; he preserved crucial shards of church doctrine—the immortal soul, for starters—while buying intellectual space for the physical sciences to continue the march toward knowledge.

In solving one problem, however, Descartes created many others, questions that have bedeviled philosophers and theologians ever since. "I am a thinking thing that can exist without a body," Descartes wrote. If that was true, then why not liberate the mind from the body's prison? Descartes tried his darndest. He conceived a philosophical method that sounded a bit like a self-help regimen. He set about writing rules to achieve a state of what he called "pure understanding" or "pure intellection." He would purge his mind of bodily urges to make way for the ideas that God had intended to occupy the mind. As Descartes instructed himself, "I shall now close my eyes, I shall stop my ears, I shall call away my senses, I shall efface even from my thoughts all images of corporeal things." This wasn't just a gambit to unleash his own mind, but a method intended to elevate humanity. The intellectual historian David Noble describes Descartes's project: "He believed that his philosophical method might help mankind overcome the epistemological handicaps of its fallen state and re-gain control of some of its innate godly powers."

Descartes's obsession became philosophy's obsession. Over the centuries, mathematicians and logicians—Gottfried Leibniz, George Boole, Alfred North Whitehead—aspired to create a new system that would express thought in its purest (and therefore most divine) form. But for all the genius of these new systems, the prison of the body remained. Philosophy couldn't emancipate the mind, but technology just might. Google has set out to suc-ceed where Descartes failed, except that it has jettisoned all the philosophical questions that rattled around in his head. Where Descartes emphasized skepticism and doubt, Google is never plagued by second-guessing. It has turned the liberation of the brain into an engineering challenge—an exercise that often fails to ask basic questions about the human implications of the proj-ect. This is a moral failing that afflicts Google and has haunted computer science from the start.

ALAN TURING WAS AN ATHEIST and a loner. He relished being an out-sider. When his mother dispatched him at age fourteen to suffer the cold-shower, hard-bed plight of his new boarding school, he bicycled alone to campus, sixty miles in two days. He could be shy and strange. To combat the hay fever that arrived every June, he would don a gas mask. His own mother wrote, "The seclusion of a medieval monastery would have suited him very well." Exacerbating his innate sense of alienation, he was gay in a society that criminalized and hounded homosexuals.

Descartes had celebrated the sort of isolation that was often Turing's fate. And indeed, his quiet moments yielded epiphany. In the words of the British philosopher Stuart Hampshire, Turing had "the gift for solitary thinking." He was capable of intense concentration that blocked received wisdom and the orthodoxies of his colleagues from infiltrating his thoughts. On a summer run in 1935, Turing lay down amid apple trees and conceived of something he called the Logical Computing Machine. His vision, recorded on paper, became the blueprint for the digital revolution.

Engineering is considered the paragon of rationality—a profession devoted to systems and planning, the enemy of spontaneity and instinct. Turing certainly enjoyed playing the role of scientific scold, gleefully mocking all those who nervously fretted over the implications of new inventions. "One day ladies will take their computers for walks in the park and tell each other 'My little computer said such a funny thing this morning!'" he quipped.

This posture was a bit rich. In his most influential essays, Turing wasn't simply reporting the evidence—or carefully deploying inductive reasoning. Once you cut through his arch wit and logical bravura, you could see he was thinking spiritually. The mathematicians and engineers may have disavowed the existence of God, but they placed themselves in a celestial role of giving life to a pile of inorganic material. And it changed them.

Turing believed that the computer wasn't just a machine, it was also a child, a being capable of learning. At times, he described his invention as if it were an English public-school boy, making progress thanks only to a healthy dose of punishment and the occasional rewards. Yet, he never did doubt its potential to achieve: "We may hope that machines will eventually compete with men in all purely intellectual fields." He wrote those words in 1950, when computers were relatively impotent, very large boxes that could do a little bit of math. At that moment, there was little evidence to justify the belief that these machines would ever acquire the capabilities of the human brain. Still, Turing had faith. He imagined a test of the computer's intelligence in which a person would send written questions to a human and a machine in another room. Receiving two sets of answers, the interrogator would have to guess which answers came from the human. Turing predicted that within fifty years the machine would routinely fool the questioner.

THIS PREDICTION SET THE TERMS for the computer age. Ever since, engineers have futilely attempted to build machines capable of passing Turing's test. For many of those seeking to invent AI, their job is just a heap of mathematics, a thrilling intellectual challenge. But for a significant chunk of others, it's a theological pursuit. They are at the center of a transformative project that will culminate in the dawning of a new age. The high priest of this religion is a rhetorically gifted, canny popularizer called Ray Kurzweil.

His ecstatic vision for the future was born in the greatest catastrophe of the past. The penumbra of the Holocaust hangs over him. His parents, Viennese Jews, fled on the eve of the Anschluss. The accretion of so many difficult years took its toll on his father, a classical conductor and intellectual. He died of a heart attack at the age of fifty-eight, a loss that never seems far from Kurzweil's mind. Like many children of parents who have seen the worst, he counteracted the grimness of history with his own willful, super-charged optimism. From the youngest age, he was seized with the spirit of invention. As a seventeen-year-old, he made an appearance on Steve Allen's game show, *I've Got a Secret*. He played the piano with virtuosity; Allen then asked the panel to guess his concealed truth. Under questioning by the show's panelists, Kurzweil finally revealed that the music he played was composed by a computer. The audience was gobsmacked by that, but not as much as by the fact that a scrawny teen from Queens had invented the machine revealed on the set. He proudly walked Allen around a noisy hulking pile of wires, flashing lights, and relays, the work of a savant.

Kurzweil was the perfect engineer, confident that he could work out any puzzle put in front of him. As a newly minted graduate of MIT, he proclaimed to a friend that he wanted "to invent things so that the blind could see, and the deaf could hear, and the lame could walk." At the age of twenty-seven, he created a machine that could read to the blind. To describe the invention hardly captures its audacity. The blind could place their book on a scanner that would then pour the text into a computer, which would then articulate the words—before Kurzweil's machine, a flatbed scanner hadn't existed.

This machine made him something of a hero to the blind, whose lives he had transformed. Stevie Wonder, for one, genuflected in Kurzweil's direction. They became friends. For the sake of his new pal, Kurzweil created a new electronic keyboard, which purportedly matched the quality of the grand pianos in the world's supreme concert halls.

For all his optimism, however, Kurzweil couldn't escape his fears—or more precisely, he couldn't escape the biggest fear of them all. His mind frequently wandered to death, such a "profoundly sad, lonely feeling that I really can't bear it." But this, too, he vowed, was a problem that engineering could solve. To prolong his own life, he began manically swallowing pills—vitamins, supplements, enzymes. One hundred fifty or so of these capsules go down his gullet daily. (He also receives a regular injection that he believes will help insulate him from the inevitable.) In a hagiographic documentary about him, we watch him as he glides through a cocktail party, a glass of red wine in hand. He pops pills, as if they were Chex Mix, while making small talk with strangers. We later learn that his ingestion is something of a product placement—he started a company, Ray and Terry's Longevity Products, that manufactures many of the tablets and elixirs that he consumes.

But pharmaceuticals are just a sideline for Kurzweil. His main business is prophecy. Kurzweil believes fervently in AI, which he studied at MIT with its earliest pioneers, and yearns for the heaven on earth it will create. This paradise has a name—it's called the singularity. Kurzweil borrowed the term from the mathematician-cum-science-fiction-writer Vernor Vinge, who, in turn, filched it from astrophysics. The singularity refers to a rupture in the time-space continuum—it describes the moment when the finite become infinite. In Kurzweil's telling, the singularity is when artificial intelligence becomes all-powerful, when computers are capable of designing and building other computers. This superintelligence will, of course, create a superintelligence even more powerful than itself—and so on, down the posthuman generations. At that point, all bets are off—"strong AI and nanotechnology can create any product, any situation, any environment that we can imagine at will."

As a scientist, Kurzweil believes in precision. When he makes predictions, he doesn't chuck darts; he extrapolates data. In fact, he's loaded everything we know about the history of human technology onto his computer and run the numbers. Technological progress, he has concluded, isn't a matter of linear growth; it's a never-ending exponential explosion. "Each epoch of evolution has progressed more rapidly by building on the products of the previous stage," he writes. Kurzweil has named this observation the Law of Accelerating Returns. And in his telling, humanity is about to place a lead foot on its technological accelerator—we're on the threshold of massive leaps in genetics, nanotechnology, and robotics. These developments will allow us to finally shed our "frail" and "limited" human bodies and brains, what he calls our "version 1.0 biological bodies." We will fully merge with machines; our existence will become virtual; our brains will be uploaded. Thanks to his scientific reading, he can tell you the singularity will dawn in the year 2045.

Humanity will finally fulfill Descartes's dreams of liberating the mind from the prison of the body. As Kurzweil puts it, "We will be software, not hardware," and able to inhabit whatever hardware we like best. There will not be any difference between us and robots. "What, after all, is the difference between a human who has upgraded her body and brain using new nanotechnology, and computational technologies, and a robot who has gained an intelligence and sensuality surpassing her human creators?"

The world will then change quickly: Computers will complete every basic human task, which will permit lives of leisure; pain will disappear, as will death; technology will solve the basic condition of scarcity that has always haunted life on the planet. Even life under the sheets will be better: "Virtual sex will provide sensations that are more intense and pleasurable than conventional sex." Humans can pretend like they have the power to alter this course, but they are fooling themselves. Peter Diamandis, one of Silicon Valley's most prestigious thinkers, puts it quite starkly: "Anybody who is going to be resisting this progress forward is going to be resisting evolution. And fundamentally they will die out."

Kurzweil is aware of the metaphysical implications of his theory. He called one of his treatises *The Age of Spiritual Machines*. His descriptions of life after the singularity are nothing short of rapturous. "Our civilization will then expand outward, turning all the dumb matter and energy we encounter into sublimely intelligent—transcendent—matter and energy. So in a sense, we can say that the Singularity will ultimately infuse the universe with spirit." Kurzweil even maintains a storage unit where he has stockpiled his father's papers, down to his financial ledgers, in anticipation of the day he can resurrect him. When the anthropologist of religion Robert Geraci studied Kurzweil and other singularitarians, he noticed how precisely their belief seemed to echo Christian apocalyptic texts. "Apocalyptic AI is the legitimate heir to these religious promises, not a bastardized version of them," he concluded. "In Apocalyptic AI, technological research and religious categories come together in a stirringly well-integrated unit."

The singularity is hardly the state religion of Silicon Valley. In some neighborhoods of techland, Kurzweil is subjected to haughty dismissal. John McCarthy, the godfather of AI, once said that he wanted to live to 102, so that he could laugh at Kurzweil when the singularity fails to arrive at its appointed hour. Still, Kurzweil's devotees include members of the tech A-list. Bill Gates, for one, calls him "the best person I know at predicting the future of artificial intelligence." The *New York Times*'s John Markoff, our most important chronicler of the technologists, says that Kurzweil "represents a community of many of Silicon Valley's best and brightest," ranks that include the finest minds at Google.

LARRY PAGE LIKES TO IMAGINE that he never escaped academia. Google, after all, began as a doctoral dissertation—and the inspiration for the search engine came from his connoisseurship of academic papers. As the son of a professor, he knew how researchers judge their own work. They look at the number of times it gets cited by other papers. His eureka moment arrived when he saw how the Web mimicked the professoriate. Links were just like citations—both were, in their way, a form of recommendation. The utility of a Web page could be judged by tabulating the number of links it received on other pages. When he captured this insight in an algorithm, he punningly named it for himself: PageRank.

Research is a pursuit Page cherishes, and in which Google invests vast sums—last year it spent nearly $12.5 billion on R&D and on projects that it won't foreseeably monetize. The company has built a revolving front door through which superstar professors regularly cycle, joining the company's most audacious ventures. If there's tension between profit and the pursuit of scientific purity, Page will make a big show of choosing the path of purity. That is, of course, a source of Google's success over the years. Where other search engines sold higher placement in their rankings, Google never took that blatantly transactional path. It could plausibly claim that its search results were scientifically derived.

This idealism is a bit for show, but it's mostly something that originates in the company's marrow. "Google is not a conventional company. We do not intend to become one," Page and Brin proclaimed in a letter that they sent to the Securities and Exchange Commission, attached to the company's initial public offering in 2004. This statement could be read as empty rhetoric, but it gave Wall Street a case of heartburn. Close observers of the company understood that Google abhorred MBA types. It stubbornly resisted the creation of a marketing department. Page prided himself on hiring engineers for business-minded jobs that would traditionally go to someone trained in, say, finance. Even as Google came to employ tens of thousands of workers, Larry Page personally reviewed a file on each potential hire to make sure that the company didn't veer too far from its engineering roots.

The best expression of the company's idealism was its oft-mocked motto, "Don't be evil." That slogan becomes easier to understand, and a more potent expression of values, when you learn that Google never intended the phrase for public consumption. The company meant to focus employees on the beneficent, ambitious mission of the company—a Post-it note to the corporate self, reminding Google not to behave as selfishly and narrow-mindedly as Microsoft, the king of tech it intended to dethrone. The aphorism became widely known only after the company's CEO, Eric Schmidt, inadvertently mentioned it in an interview with *Wired*, an act of blabbing that frustrated many in the company, who understood how the motto would make Google a slow-moving target for ridicule. (Google eventually retired the motto.) When Larry Page issues his pronouncements, they are unusually earnest. And the talking points that he repeats often are a good measure of his true, supersized intentions. He has a talent for sentences that are at once self-effacing and impossibly grandiose: "We're at maybe 1% of what is possible. Despite the faster change, we're still moving slow relative to the opportunities we have."

To understand Page's intentions, it's necessary to examine the varieties of artificial intelligence. The field can be roughly divided in two. There's a school of incrementalists, who cherish everything that has been accomplished to date—victories like the Page-Rank algorithm or the software that allows ATMs to read the scrawled writing on checks. This school holds out little to no hope that computers will ever acquire anything approximating human consciousness. Then there are the revolutionaries who gravitate toward Kurzweil and the singularitarian view. They aim to build computers with either "artificial general intelligence" or "strong AI."

For most of Google's history, it trained its efforts on incremental improvements. During that earlier era, the company was run by Eric Schmidt—an older, experienced manager, whom Google's investors forced Page and Brin to accept as their "adult" supervisor. That's not to say that Schmidt was timid. Those years witnessed Google's plot to upload every book on the planet and the creation of products that are now commonplace utilities, like Gmail, Google Docs, and Google Maps.

But those ambitions never stretched quite far enough to satisfy Larry Page. In 2011, Page shifted himself back into the corner office, the CEO job he held at Google's birth. And he redirected the company toward singularitarian goals. Over the years, he had befriended Kurzweil and worked with him on assorted projects. After he returned to his old job, Page hired Kurzweil and anointed him Google's director of engineering. He assigned him the task of teaching computers to read—the sort of exponential breakthrough that would hasten the arrival of the superintelligence that Kurzweil celebrates. "This is the culmination of literally 50 years of my focus on artificial intelligence," Kurzweil said upon signing up with Google.

When you listen to Page talk to his employees, he returns time and again to the metaphor of the moonshot. The company has an Apollolike program for reaching artificial general intelligence: a project called Google Brain, a moniker with creepy implications. ("The Google policy on a lot of things is to get right up to the creepy line and not cross it," Eric Schmidt has quipped.) Google has spearheaded the revival of a concept first explored in the sixties, one that has failed until recently: neural networks, which involve computing modeled on the workings of the human brain. Algorithms replicate the brain's information processing and its methods for learning. Google has hired the British-born professor Geoff Hinton, who has made the greatest progress in this direction. It also acquired a London-based company called DeepMind, which created neural networks that taught themselves, without human instruction, to play video games. Because DeepMind feared the dangers of a single company possessing such powerful algorithms, it insisted that Google never permit its work to be militarized or sold to intelligence services.

How deeply does Google believe in the singularity? Hardly everyone in the company agrees with Kurzweil's vision. One of the company's most accomplished engineers, Peter Norvig, has argued against the Law of Accelerating Returns. And Larry Page has never publicly commented on Kurzweil. Yet, there's an undeniable pattern. In 2008 Google helped bankroll the creation of Singularity University, housed on a NASA campus in Silicon Valley—a ten-week "graduate" program cofounded by Kurzweil to promote his ideas. Google has donated millions so that students can attend SU on a free ride. "If I were a student, this is where I would like to be," Page has said. The company has indulged a slew of singularitarian obsessions. It has, for instance, invested heavily in Calico, a start-up that wants to solve the problem of death, as opposed to tackling comparatively trivial issues like cancer. "One of the things I thought was amazing is that if you solve cancer, you'd add about three years to people's average life expectancy," Page said in an interview with *Time*. "We think of solving cancer as this huge thing that'll totally change the world. But when you really take a step back and look at it, yeah, there are many, many tragic cases of cancer, and it's very, very sad, but in the aggregate, it's not as big an advance as you might think." Google will likely achieve very few of its goals—moonshot will prove scattershot. Still, these projects reveal a worldview, a stunningly coherent set of values and beliefs.

The singularity isn't just a vision of the future. It implies a view of the present. According to Larry Page's Panglossian theory of life on planet Earth, we're getting achingly close to a world devoid of scarcity and brimming with wonders—the stakes are such that we would be foolish, unfeeling even, not to hasten the arrival of this new day. Some are blind to the possibilities, out of Luddism or narrowness of imagination. But that's the nature of scientific revolutions; they are propelled by heretics and rule-breakers. This intense mission is driven by arrogance and a rather shocking carelessness. In its pursuit of the future, Google often finds itself pondering and developing technologies that will significantly alter long-standing human practices. Its approach is to barrel forward with alacrity, confident in its own goodness.

When the company decided to digitize every book in existence, it considered copyright law a trivial annoyance, hardly worth a moment's hesitation. Of course, Google must have had an inkling of how its project would be perceived. That's why it went about its mission quietly, to avoid scrutiny. "There was a cloak-and-dagger element to the procedure, soured by a clandestine taint," Steven Levy recounts of the effort, "like ducking out of a 1950s nightclub to smoke weed." Google's trucks would pull up to libraries and quietly walk away with boxes of books to be quickly scanned and returned. "If you don't have a reason to talk about it, why talk about it?" Larry Page would argue, when confronted with pleas to publicly announce the existence of its program. The company's lead lawyer on this described bluntly the roughshod attitude of his colleagues: "Google's leadership doesn't care terribly much about precedent or law." In this case precedent was the centuries-old protections of intellectual property, and the consequences were a potential devastation of the publishing industry and all the writers who depend on it. In other words, Google had plotted an intellectual heist of historic proportions.

What motivated Google in its pursuit? On one level, the answer is clear: To maintain dominance, Google's search engine must be definitive. Here was a massive store of human knowledge waiting to be stockpiled and searched. On the other hand, there are less obvious motives: When the historian of technology George Dyson visited the Googleplex to give a talk, an engineer casually admitted, "We are not scanning all those books to be read by people. We are scanning them to be read by an AI." If that's true, then it's easier to understand Google's secrecy. The world's greatest collection of knowledge was mere grist to train machines, a sacrifice for the singularity.

Google is a company without clear boundaries, or rather, a company with ever-expanding boundaries. That's why it's chilling to hear Larry Page denounce competition as a wasteful concept and to hear him celebrate cooperation as the way forward. "Being negative is not how we make progress and most important things are not zero sum," he says. "How exciting is it to come to work if the best you can do is trounce some other company that does roughly the same thing?" And it's even more chilling to hear him contemplate how Google will someday employ more than one million people, a company twenty times larger than it is now. That's not just a boast about dominating an industry where he faces no true rivals, it's a boast about dominating something far vaster, a statement of Google's intent to impose its values and theological convictions on the world.

Three

MARK ZUCKERBERG'S WAR ON FREE WILL

SILICON VALLEY GRADUATED from the counterculture, but not really. All the values it professes are the values of the sixties. The big tech companies present themselves as platforms for personal liberation, just as Stewart Brand preached. Everyone has the right to speak their mind on social media, to fulfill their intellectual and democratic potential, to express their individuality. Where television had been a passive medium that rendered citizens inert, Facebook is participatory and empowering. It allows users to read widely, think for themselves, and form their own opinions.

We can't entirely dismiss this rhetoric. There are parts of the world, even in the United States, where Facebook emboldens citizens and enables them to organize themselves in opposition to power. But we shouldn't accept Facebook's self-conception as sincere, either. Facebook is a carefully managed top-down system, not a robust public square. It mimics some of the patterns of conversation, but that's a surface trait. In reality, Facebook is a tangle of rules and procedures for sorting information, rules devised by the corporation for the ultimate benefit of the corporation. Facebook is always surveilling users, always auditing them, using them as lab rats in its behavioral experiments. While it creates the impression that it offers choice, Facebook paternalistically nudges users in the direction it deems best for them, which also happens to be the direction that thoroughly addicts them. It's a phoniness most obvious in the compressed, historic career of Facebook's mastermind.

MARK ZUCKERBERG IS A GOOD BOY, but he wanted to be bad, or maybe just a little bit naughty. The heroes of his adolescence were the original hackers. Let's be precise about the term. His idols weren't malevolent data thieves or cyber-terrorists. In the parlance of hacker culture, such ill-willed outlaws are known as crackers. Zuckerberg never put crackers on a pedestal. Still, his hacker heroes were disrespectful of authority. They were technically virtuosic, infinitely resourceful nerd cowboys, unbound by conventional thinking. In MIT's labs, during the sixties and seventies, they broke any rule that interfered with building the stuff of early computing, such marvels as the first video games and word processors. With their free time, they played epic pranks, which happened to draw further attention to their own cleverness—installing a living, breathing cow on the roof of a Cambridge dorm; launching a weather balloon, which miraculously emerged from beneath the turf, emblazoned with "MIT," in the middle of a Harvard-Yale football game.

The hackers' archenemies were the bureaucrats who ran universities, corporations, and governments. Bureaucrats talked about making the world more efficient, just like the hackers. But they were really small-minded paper-pushers who fiercely guarded the information they held, even when that information yearned to be shared. When hackers clearly engineered better ways of doing things—a box that enabled free long-distance calls, an instruction that might improve an operating system—the bureaucrats stood in their way, wagging an unbending finger. The hackers took aesthetic and comic pleasure in outwitting the men in suits.

When Zuckerberg arrived at Harvard in the fall of 2002, the heyday of the hackers had long passed. They were older guys now, the stuff of good tales, some stuck in twilight struggles against The Man. But Zuckerberg wanted to hack, too, and with that old-time indifference to norms. In high school—using the *nom de hack* Zuck Fader—he picked the lock that prevented outsiders from fiddling with AOL's code and added his own improvements to its instant messaging program. As a college sophomore he hatched a site called Facemash—with the high-minded purpose of determining the hottest kid on campus. Zuckerberg asked users to compare images of two students and then determine the better looking of the two. The winner of each pairing advanced to the next round of his hormonal tournament. To cobble this site together, Zuckerberg needed photos. He purloined those from the servers of the various Harvard houses that stockpiled them. "One thing is certain," he wrote on a blog as he put the finishing touches on his creation, "and it's that I'm a jerk for making this site. Oh well."

His brief experimentation with rebellion ended with his apologizing to a Harvard disciplinary panel, as well as campus women's groups, and mulling strategies to redeem his soiled reputation. In the years since, he's shown that defiance really wasn't his natural inclination. His distrust of authority was such that he sought out Don Graham, then the venerable chairman of the Washington Post company, as his mentor. After he started Facebook, he shadowed various giants of corporate America so that he could study their managerial styles up close. Though he hasn't fully shed his awkward ways, he has sufficiently overcome his introversion to appear at fancy dinner parties, Charlie Rose interviews, and *Vanity Fair* cover shoots.

Still, the juvenile fascination with hackers never did die, or rather he carried it forward into his new, more mature incarnation. When he finally had a corporate campus of his own, he procured a vanity address for it: One Hacker Way. He designed a plaza with h-a-c-k inlaid into the concrete. In the center of his office park, he created an open meeting space called Hacker Square. This is, of course, the venue where his employees join for all-night Hackathons. As he told a group of would-be entrepreneurs, "We've got this whole ethos that we want to build a hacker culture."

Plenty of companies have similarly appropriated hacker culture—hackers are the ur-disrupters—but none have gone as far as Facebook. Of course, that's not without risks. "Hacking" is a loaded term, and a potentially alienating one, at least to shareholders who crave sensible rule-abiding leadership. But by the time Zuckerberg began extolling the virtues of hacking, he'd stripped the name of most of its original meaning and distilled it into a managerial philosophy that contains barely a hint of rebelliousness. It might even be the opposite of rebelliousness. Hackers, he told one interviewer, were "just this group of computer scientists who were trying to quickly prototype and see what was possible. That's what I try to encourage our engineers to do here."

To hack is to be a good worker, a responsible Facebook citizen—a microcosm of the way in which the company has taken the language of radical individualism and deployed it in the service of conformism.

Zuckerberg claimed to have distilled that hacker spirit into a motivational motto: "Move Fast and Break Things." Indeed, Facebook has excelled at that. The truth is, Facebook moved faster than Zuckerberg could ever have imagined. He hadn't really intended his creation. His company was, as we all know, a dorm room lark, a thing he ginned up in a Red Bull–induced fit of sleeplessness. As his creation grew, it needed to justify its new scale to its investors, to its users, to the world. It needed to grow up fast. According to Dustin Moskovitz, who cofounded the company with Zuckerberg at Harvard, "It was always very important for our brand to get away from the image of frivolity it had, especially in Silicon Valley." Over the span of its short life, the company has caromed from self-description to self-description. It has called itself a tool, a utility, and a platform. It has talked about openness and connectedness. And in all these attempts at defining itself, it has managed to clarify its intentions.

Though Facebook will occasionally talk about the transparency of governments and corporations, what it really wants to advance is the transparency of individuals—or what it has called, at various moments, "radical transparency" or "ultimate transparency." The theory holds that the sunshine of sharing our intimate details will disinfect the moral mess of our lives. Even if we don't intend for our secrets to become public knowledge, their exposure will improve society. With the looming threat that our embarrassing information will be broadcast, we'll behave better. And perhaps the ubiquity of incriminating photos and damning revelations will prod us to become more tolerant of one another's sins. Besides, there's virtue in living our lives truthfully. "The days of you having a different image for your work friends or co-workers and for the other people you know are probably coming to an end pretty quickly," Zuckerberg has said. "Having two identities for yourself is an example of a lack of integrity."

The point is that Facebook has a strong, paternalistic view on what's best for you, and it's trying to transport you there. "To get people to this point where there's more openness—that's a big challenge. But I think we'll do it," Zuckerberg has said. He has reason to believe that he will achieve that goal. With its size, Facebook has amassed outsized powers. These powers are so great that Zuckerberg doesn't bother denying that fact. "In a lot of ways Facebook is more like a government than a traditional company. We have this large community of people, and more than other technology companies we're really setting policies."

WITHOUT KNOWING IT, Zuckerberg is the heir to a long political tradition. Over the last two hundred years, the West has been unable to shake an abiding fantasy, a dream sequence in which we throw out the bum politicians and replace them with engineers—rule by slide rule. The French were the first to entertain this notion in the bloody, world-churning aftermath of their revolution. A coterie of the country's most influential philosophers (notably, Henri de Saint-Simon and Auguste Comte) were genuinely torn about the course of the country. They hated all the old ancient bastions of parasitic power—the feudal lords, the priests, and the warriors—but they also feared the chaos of the mob. To split the difference, they proposed a form of technocracy—engineers and assorted technicians would rule with beneficent disinterestedness. Engineers would strip the old order of its power, while governing in the spirit of science. They would impose rationality and order.

This dream has captivated intellectuals ever since, especially Americans. The great sociologist Thorstein Veblen was obsessed with installing engineers in power and, in 1921, wrote a book making his case. His vision briefly became a reality. In the aftermath of World War I, American elites were aghast at all the irrational impulses unleashed by that conflict—the xenophobia, the racism, the urge to lynch and riot. What's more, the realities of economic life had grown so complicated, how could politicians possibly manage them? Americans of all persuasions began yearning for the salvific ascendance of the most famous engineer of his time: Herbert Hoover. During the war, Hoover had organized a system that managed to feed starving Europe, despite the seeming impossibility of that assignment. In 1920, Franklin Roosevelt—who would, of course, ultimately vanquish him from politics—organized a movement to draft Hoover for the presidency.

The Hoover experiment, in the end, hardly realized the happy fantasies about the Engineer King. A very different version of this dream, however, has come to fruition, in the form of the CEOs of the big tech companies. We're not ruled by engineers, not yet, but they have become the dominant force in American life, the highest, most influential tier of our elite. Marc Andreessen coined a famous aphorism that holds, "Software is eating the world." There's a bit of obfuscation in that formula—it's really the authors of software who are eating the world.

There's another way to describe this historical progression. Automation has come in waves. During the Industrial Revolution, machinery replaced manual workers. At first machines required human operators. Over time, machines came to function with hardly any human intervention. For centuries, engineers automated physical labor; our new engineering elite has automated thought. They have perfected technologies that take over intellectual processes, that render the brain redundant. Or as Marissa Mayer once argued, "You have to make *words* less human and more a piece of the *machine*." Indeed, we have begun to outsource our intellectual work to companies that suggest what we should learn, the topics we should consider, and the items we ought to buy. These companies can justify their incursions into our lives with the very arguments that Saint-Simon and Comte articulated: They are supplying us with efficiency; they are imposing order on human life.

Nobody better articulates the modern faith in engineering's power to transform society than Zuckerberg. He told a group of software developers, "You know, I'm an engineer, and I think a key part of the engineering mindset is this hope and this belief that you can take any system that's out there and make it much, much better than it is today. Anything, whether it's hardware, or software, a company, a developer ecosystem, you can take anything and make it much, much better." The world will improve, if only Zuckerberg's reason can prevail—and it will.

THE PRECISE SOURCE OF FACEBOOK'S power is algorithms. That's a concept repeated dutifully in nearly every story about the tech giants, yet it remains fuzzy at best to users of those sites. From the moment of the algorithm's invention, it was possible to see its power, its revolutionary potential. The algorithm was developed in order to automate thinking, to remove difficult decisions from the hands of humans, to settle contentious debates. To understand the essence of the algorithm—and its utopian pretension—it's necessary to travel back to its birthplace, the brain of one of history's unimpeachable geniuses, Gottfried Leibniz.

Fifty years younger than Descartes, Leibniz grew up in the same world of religious conflict. His native Germany, Martin Luther's homeland, had become one of history's most horrific abattoirs, the contested territory at the center of the Thirty Years War. Although the battlefield made its own contribution to the corpse count, the aftermath of war was terrible, too. Dysentery, typhus, and plague conquered the German principalities. Famine and demographic collapse followed battle, some four million deaths in total. The worst-clobbered of the German states lost more than half of their population.

Leibniz was born as Europe negotiated the Peace of Westphalia ending the slaughter, so it was inevitable that he trained his prodigious intellectual energies on reconciling Protestants and Catholics, crafting schemes to unify humanity. Prodigious is perhaps an inadequate term to describe Leibniz's mental reserves. He produced schemes at, more or less, the rate he contracted his diaphragm. His archives, which still haven't been fully published, contain some two hundred thousand pages of his writing, filled with spectacular creations. Leibniz invented calculus—to be sure, he hadn't realized that Newton discovered the subject earlier, but it's his notation that we still use. He produced lasting treatises on metaphysics and theology, he drew up designs for watches and windmills, he advocated universal health care and the development of submarines. As a diplomat in Paris, he pressed Louis XIV to invade Egypt, a bank-shot ploy to divert Germany's mighty neighbor into an overseas adventure that might lessen the prospect of marching its armies east. Denis Diderot, no slouch, moaned, "When one compares . . . one's own small talents with those of a Leibniz, one is tempted to throw away one's books and go die peacefully in the depths of some dark corner."

Of all Leibniz's schemes, the dearest was a new lexicon he called the universal characteristic—and it, too, sprang from his desire for peace. Throughout history, fanciful thinkers have created languages from scratch in the hope that their concoctions would smooth communication between the peoples of the world, fostering the preconditions for global oneness. Leibniz created his language for that reason, too, but he also had higher hopes: He argued that a new set of symbols and expressions would lead science and philosophy to new truths, to a new age of reason, to a deeper appreciation of the universe's elegance and harmony, to the divine.

What he imagined was an alphabet of human thought. It was an idea that he first pondered as a young student, the basis for his doctoral dissertation at Altdorf. Over the years, he fleshed out a detailed plan for realizing his fantasy. A group of scholars would create an encyclopedia containing the fundamental, incontestably true concepts of the world, of physics, philosophy, geometry, everything really. He called these core concepts "primitives," and they would include things like the earth, the color red, and God. Each of the primitives would be assigned a numerical value, which allowed them to be combined to create new concepts or to express complex extant ones. And those numerical values would form the basis for a new calculus of thought, what he called the calculus ratiocinator.

Leibniz illustrated his scheme with an example. What is a

human? A rational animal, of course. That's an insight that we can write like this:

rational x animal = man

But Leibniz translated this expression into an even more mathematical sentence. "Animal," he suggested, might be represented with the number two; "rational" with the number three. Therefore:

2 x 3 = 6

Thought had been turned into math—and this allowed for a new, foolproof method for adjudicating questions of truth. Leibniz asked, for instance, are all men monkeys? Well, he knew the number assigned to monkeys, ten. If ten can't be divided by six, and six can't be divided by ten, then we know: There's no element of monkey in man—and no element of man in monkey.

That was the point of his language: Knowledge, all knowledge, could ultimately be derived from computation. It would be an effortless process, *cogitatio caeca* or blind thought. Humans were no longer even needed to conceive new ideas. A machine could do that, by combining and dividing concepts. In fact, Leibniz built a prototype of such a machine, a gorgeous, intricate compilation of polished brass and steel, gears and dials. He called it the Stepped Reckoner. Leibniz spent a personal fortune building it. With a turn of the crank in one direction the Stepped Reckoner could multiply, in the other direction divide. Leibniz had designed a user interface so meticulous that Steve Jobs would have bowed down before it. Sadly, whenever he tested the machine for an audience, as he did before the Royal Society in London in 1673; it failed. The resilient Leibniz forgave himself these humiliating demonstrations. The importance of the universal characteristic demanded that he press forward. "Once this has been done, if ever further controversies should arise, there should be no more reason for disputes between two philosophers than between two calculators." Intellectual and moral argument could be settled with the disagreeing parties declaring, "Let's calculate!" There would be no need for wars, let alone theological controversy, because truth would be placed on the terra firma of math.

Leibniz was a prophet of the digital age, though his pregnant ideas sat in the waiting room for centuries. He proposed a numeric system that used only zeros and ones, the very system of binary on which computing rests. He explained how automation of white-collar jobs would enhance productivity. But his critical insight was mechanical thinking, the automation of reason, the very thing that makes the Internet so miraculous, and the power of the tech companies so potentially menacing.

THOSE PROCEDURES THAT enable mechanical thinking came to have a name. They were dubbed algorithms. The essence of the algorithm is entirely uncomplicated. The textbooks compare them to recipes—a series of precise steps that can be followed mindlessly. This is different from equations, which have one correct result. Algorithms merely capture the process for solving a problem and say nothing about where those steps ultimately lead.

These recipes are the crucial building blocks of software. Programmers can't simply order a computer to, say, search the Internet. They must give the computer a set of specific instructions for accomplishing that task. These instructions must take the messy human activity of looking for information and transpose that into an orderly process that can be expressed in code. First do this . . . then do that. . . . The process of translation, from concept to procedure to code, is inherently reductive. Complex processes must be subdivided into a series of binary choices. There's no equation to suggest a dress to wear, but an algorithm could easily be written for that—it will work its way through a series of either/or questions (morning or night, winter or summer, sun or rain), with each choice pushing to the next.

Mechanical thinking was exactly what Alan Turing first imagined as he collapsed on his run through the meadows of Cambridge in 1935 and daydreamed about a fantastical new calculating machine. For the first decades of computing, the term "algorithm" wasn't much mentioned. But as computer science departments began sprouting across campuses in the sixties, the term acquired a new cachet. Its vogue was the product of status anxiety. Programmers, especially in the academy, were anxious to show that they weren't mere technicians. They began to describe their work as algorithmic, in part because it tied them to one of the greatest of all mathematicians—the Persian polymath Muḥammad ibn Mūsā al-Khwārizmi, or as he was known in Latin, Algoritmi. During the twelfth century, translations of al-Khwārizmi introduced Arabic numerals to the West; his treatises pioneered algebra and trigonometry. By describing the algorithm as the fundamental element of programming, the computer scientists were attaching themselves to a grand history. It was a savvy piece of name dropping: See, we're not arriviste, we're working with abstractions and theories, just like the mathematicians!

There was sleight of hand in this self-portrayal. The algorithm may be the essence of computer science—but it's not precisely a scientific concept. An algorithm is a system, like plumbing or a military chain of command. It takes know-how, calculation, and creativity to make a system work properly. But some systems, like some armies, are much more reliable than others. A system is a human artifact, not a mathematical truism. The origins of the algorithm are unmistakably human, but human fallibility isn't a quality that we associate with it. When algorithms reject a loan application or set the price for an airline flight, they seem impersonal and unbending. The algorithm is supposed to be devoid of bias, intuition, emotion, or forgiveness. They call it a search engine, after all—a nod to pistons, gears, and twentieth-century industry, with the machinery wiped clean of human fingerprints.

Silicon Valley's algorithmic enthusiasts were immodest about describing the revolutionary potential of their objects of affection. Algorithms were always interesting and valuable, but advances in computing made them infinitely more powerful. The big change was the cost of computing. It collapsed, and just as the machines themselves sped up and were tied into a global network. Computers could stockpile massive piles of unsorted data—and algorithms could attack this data to find patterns and connections that would escape human analysts. In the hands of Google and Facebook, these algorithms grew ever more powerful. As they went about their searches, they accumulated more and more data. Their machines assimilated all the lessons of past searches, using these learnings to more precisely deliver the desired results.

For the entirety of human existence, the creation of knowledge was a slog of trial and error. Humans would dream up theories of how the world worked, then would examine the evidence to see whether their hypotheses survived or crashed upon their exposure to reality. Algorithms upend the scientific method—the patterns emerge from the data, from correlations, unguided by hypotheses. They remove humans from the whole process of inquiry. Writing in *Wired*, Chris Anderson argued: "We can stop looking for models. We can analyze the data without hypotheses about what it might show. We can throw the numbers into the biggest computing clusters the world has ever seen and let statistical algorithms find patterns where science cannot."

On one level, this is undeniable. Algorithms can translate languages without understanding words, simply by uncovering the patterns that undergird the construction of sentences. They can find coincidences that humans might never even think to seek. Walmart's algorithms found that people desperately buy strawberry Pop-Tarts as they prepare for massive storms. Still, even as an algorithm mindlessly implements its procedures—and even as it learns to see new patterns in the data—it reflects the minds of its creators, the motives of its trainers. Both Amazon and Netflix use algorithms to make recommendations about books and films. (One-third of purchases on Amazon come from these recommendations.) These algorithms seek to understand our tastes, and the tastes of like-minded consumers of culture. Yet the algorithms make fundamentally different recommendations. Amazon steers you to the sorts of books that you've seen before. Netflix directs users to the unfamiliar. There's a business reason for this difference. Blockbuster movies cost Netflix more to stream. Greater profit arrives when you decide to watch more obscure fare. Computer scientists have an aphorism that describes how algorithms relentlessly hunt for patterns: They talk about torturing the data until it confesses. Yet this metaphor contains unexamined implications. Data, like victims of torture, tells its interrogator what it wants to hear.

Sometimes, the algorithm reflects the subconscious of its creators. To take an extreme example: The Harvard professor Latanya Sweeney conducted a study that found that users with African American names were frequently targeted with Google ads that bluntly suggested that they had arrest records in need of expunging. ("Latisha Smith, Arrested?") Google is not particularly forthright about why such results appear. Their algorithm is a ferociously guarded secret. Yet, we know that Google has explicitly built its search engine to reflect values that it holds dear. It believes that the popularity of a Web site gives a good sense of its utility; it chooses to suppress pornography in its search results and not, say, anti-Semitic conspiracists; it believes that users will benefit from finding recent articles more than golden oldies. These are legitimate choices—and perhaps wise business decisions—but they are choices, not science.

Like economics, computer science has its preferred models and implicit assumptions about the world. When programmers are taught algorithmic thinking, they are told to venerate efficiency as a paramount consideration. This is perfectly understandable. An algorithm with an ungainly number of steps will gum up the machinery, and a molasseslike server is a useless one. But efficiency is also a value. When we speed things up, we're necessarily cutting corners, we're generalizing.

Algorithms can be gorgeous expressions of logical thinking, not to mention a source of ease and wonder. They can track down copies of obscure nineteenth-century tomes in a few milliseconds; they put us in touch with long-lost elementary school friends;

they enable retailers to deliver packages to our doors in a flash. Very soon, they will guide self-driving cars and pinpoint cancers growing in our innards. But to do all these things, algorithms are constantly taking our measure. They make decisions about us and on our behalf. The problem is that when we outsource thinking to machines, we are really outsourcing thinking to the organizations that run the machines.

MARK ZUCKERBERG DISINGENUOUSLY POSES as a friendly critic of algorithms. That's how he implicitly contrasts Facebook with his rivals across the way at Google. Over in Larry Page's shop, the algorithm is king, a cold, pulseless ruler. There's not a trace of life force in its recommendations and very little apparent understanding of the person keying a query into its engine. Facebook, in his flattering self-portrait, is a respite from this increasingly automated, atomistic world. "Every product you use is better off with your friends," he says.

What he is referring to is Facebook's News Feed. Here's a brief explanation for the sliver of humanity who have apparently resisted Facebook: The News Feed provides a reverse chronological index of all the status updates, articles, and photos that your friends have posted to Facebook. The News Feed is meant to be fun, but also geared to solve one of the essential problems of modernity—our inability to sift through the ever-growing, always-looming mounds of information. Who better, the theory goes, to recommend what we should read and watch than our friends? Zuckerberg has boasted that the News Feed turned Facebook into a "personalized newspaper."

Unfortunately, our friends can do only so much to winnow

things for us. Turns out, they like to share a lot. If we just read their musings and followed links to articles, we might be only a little less overwhelmed than before, or perhaps even deeper underwater. So Facebook makes its own choices about what should be read. The company's algorithms sort the thousands of things a Facebook user could possibly see down to a smaller batch of choice items. And then within those few dozen items, it decides what we might like to read first.

Algorithms are, by definition, invisibilia. But we can usually sense their presence—that somewhere in the distance, we're interacting with a machine. That's what makes Facebook's algorithm so powerful. Many users—60 percent, according to the best research—are completely unaware of its existence. But even if they know of its influence, it wouldn't really matter. Facebook's algorithm couldn't be more opaque. When the company concedes its existence to reporters, it manages to further cloud the algorithm in impenetrable descriptions. We know, for instance, that its algorithm was once called EdgeRank. But Facebook no longer uses that term. It's appropriate that the algorithm doesn't have a name. It has grown into an almost unknowable tangle of sprawl. The algorithm interprets more than one hundred thousand "signals" to make its decisions about what users see. Some of these signals apply to all Facebook users; some reflect users' particular habits and the habits of their friends. Perhaps Facebook no longer fully understands its own tangle of algorithms—the code, all sixty million lines of it, is a palimpsest, where engineers add layer upon layer of new commands. (This is hardly a condition unique to Facebook. The Cornell University computer scientist Jon Kleinberg cowrote an essay that argued, "We have, perhaps for the first time ever, built machines we do not understand. . . . At some deep level we don't even really understand how they're producing the behavior we observe. This is the essence of their incomprehensibility." What's striking is that the "we" in that sentence refers to the creators of code.)

Pondering the abstraction of this algorithm, imagine one of those earliest computers with its nervously blinking lights and long rows of dials. To tweak the algorithm, the engineers turn the knob a click or two. The engineers are constantly making small adjustments, here and there, so that the machine performs to their satisfaction. With even the gentlest caress of the metaphorical dial, Facebook changes what its users see and read. It can make our friends' photos more or less ubiquitous; it can punish posts filled with self-congratulatory musings and banish what it deems to be hoaxes; it can promote video rather than text; it can favor articles from the likes of the *New York Times* or BuzzFeed, if it so desires. Or if we want to be melodramatic about it, we could say Facebook is constantly tinkering with how its users view the world—always tinkering with the quality of news and opinion that it allows to break through the din, adjusting the quality of political and cultural discourse in order to hold the attention of users for a few more beats.

But how do the engineers know which dial to twist and how hard? There's a whole discipline, data science, to guide the writing and revision of algorithms. Facebook has a team, poached from academia, to conduct experiments on users. It's a statistician's sexiest dream—some of the largest data sets in human history, the ability to run trials on mathematically meaningful cohorts. When Cameron Marlow, the former head of Facebook's data science team, described the opportunity, he began twitching with ecstatic joy. "For the first time," Marlow said, "we have a microscope that not only lets us examine social behavior at a very fine level that we've never been able to see before but allows us to run experiments that millions of users are exposed to."

Facebook likes to boast of the fact of its experimentation more than the details of the actual experiments themselves. But there are examples that have escaped the confines of its laboratories. We know, for example, that Facebook sought to discover whether emotions are contagious. To conduct this trial, Facebook attempted to manipulate the mental state of its users. For one group, Facebook excised the positive words from the posts in the News Feed; for another group, it removed the negative words. Each group, it concluded, wrote posts that echoed the mood of the posts it had reworded. This study was roundly condemned as invasive, but it is not so unusual. As one member of Facebook's data science team confessed: "Anyone on that team could run a test. They're always trying to alter people's behavior."

There's no doubting the emotional and psychological power possessed by Facebook—at least Facebook doesn't doubt it. It has bragged about how it increased voter turnout (and organ donation) by subtly amping up the social pressures that compel virtuous behavior. Facebook has even touted the results from these experiments in peer-reviewed journals: "It is possible that more of the .60% growth in turnout between 2006 and 2010 might have been caused by a single message on Facebook." No other company has so precisely boasted about its ability to shape democracy like this—and for good reason. It's too much power to entrust to a corporation.

The many Facebook experiments add up. The company believes that it has unlocked social psychology and acquired a deeper understanding of its users than they possess of themselves.

Facebook can predict users' race, sexual orientation, relationship status, and drug use on the basis of their "likes" alone. It's Zuckerberg's fantasy that this data might be analyzed to uncover the mother of all revelations, "a fundamental mathematical law underlying human social relationships that governs the balance of who and what we all care about." That is, of course, a goal in the distance. In the meantime, Facebook will probe—constantly testing to see what we crave and what we ignore, a never-ending campaign to improve Facebook's capacity to give us the things that we want and things that we don't even know we want. Whether the information is true or concocted, authoritative reporting or conspiratorial opinion, doesn't really seem to matter much to Facebook. The crowd gets what it wants and deserves.

THE AUTOMATION OF THINKING: We're in the earliest days of this revolution, of course. But we can see where it's heading. Algorithms have retired many of the bureaucratic, clerical duties once performed by humans—and they will soon begin to replace more creative tasks. At Netflix, algorithms suggest the genres of movies to commission. Some news wires use algorithms to write stories about crime, baseball games, and earthquakes, the most rote journalistic tasks. Algorithms have produced fine art and composed symphonic music, or at least approximations of them.

It's a terrifying trajectory, especially for those of us in these lines of work. If algorithms can replicate the process of creativity, then there's little reason to nurture human creativity. Why bother with the tortuous, inefficient process of writing or painting if a computer can produce something seemingly as good and in a painless flash? Why nurture the overinflated market for high culture, when it could be so abundant and cheap? No human endeavor has resisted automation, so why should creative endeavors be any different?

The engineering mind-set has little patience for the fetishization of words and images, for the mystique of art, for moral complexity and emotional expression. It views humans as data, components of systems, abstractions. That's why Facebook has so few qualms about performing rampant experiments on its users. The whole effort is to make human beings predictable—to anticipate their behavior, which makes them easier to manipulate. With this sort of cold-blooded thinking, so divorced from the contingency and mystery of human life, it's easy to see how long-standing values begin to seem like an annoyance—why a concept like privacy would carry so little weight in the engineer's calculus, why the inefficiencies of publishing and journalism seem so imminently disruptable.

Facebook would never put it this way, but algorithms are meant to erode free will, to relieve humans of the burden of choosing, to nudge them in the right direction. Algorithms fuel a sense of omnipotence, the condescending belief that our behavior can be altered, without our even being aware of the hand guiding us, in a superior direction. That's always been a danger of the engineering mind-set, as it moves beyond its roots in building inanimate stuff and begins to design a more perfect social world. We are the screws and rivets in the grand design.

Four

JEFF BEZOS DISRUPTS KNOWLEDGE

THE GLOWING AMBITIONS OF FACEBOOK, Google, and Amazon—their sci-fi fantasies about everlasting life, their drones, their virtual realities—distract from the core basis for their dominance. These companies are our primary portals to information and knowledge. The tech monopolists take the bounty of the Internet, that decentralized mess of words and images, and turn it into something approachable and useful.

Organizing knowledge is an ancient pursuit. Those who toiled in this field over the centuries—librarians and bookstore owners, scholars and archivists—were trained to go about their work lovingly, almost worshipfully. A professional code implored them to treat their cargo as if the world depended on its safe transit through the generations. The tech companies share none of that concern. They have presided over the collapse of the economic value of knowledge, which has severely weakened newspapers, magazines, and book publishers. By collapsing the value of knowledge, they have diminished the quality of it.

It's commonly argued that they don't really deserve blame for this demise. According to this strain of conventional wisdom, it was inevitable that the price of knowledge would evaporate in the presence of the Internet. That narrative casts these companies as innocent bystanders, when, in fact, they were active, brutal accomplices. To build their empires, they targeted the weak economic underpinnings of knowledge and they knocked them right out. It was Jeff Bezos who pioneered this approach, even before the Internet had begun to truly take form—and he chose the most unlikely starting place.

BOOKSTORES PLAY AN INDISPENSABLE ROLE in our capitalist system. They are an employment program for failed graduate students; they show how low margins and bake-sale profits will not defeat the spirit of entrepreneurship. Anyone who has browsed the literary theory aisle or studied the analytics for Russian novels can surely see how the road to the economy's commanding heights begins with bookselling. Perhaps it took a visionary to understand the untapped profit potential of the book. And to be sure, only Jeff Bezos could see how the ancient technology of inking words onto deceased vegetation was the ideal vehicle for winning the Internet, a gambit for dislodging and then surpassing Walmart as the king of retail.

You might think that only an intellectual would be deluded enough to have such faith in bookselling. But that's not quite Bezos. Though he will occasionally tout a book he finds stirring, the literary and political power of his wares have never really transfixed him. In fact, he didn't especially care for the objects that would launch him on his way to fortune: "I'm grumpy when I'm forced to read a physical book because it's not as convenient. Turning the pages . . . the book is always flopping itself shut at the wrong moment."

When he first pondered Amazon in 1994, he was a hotshot at a boutique hedge fund. He had the logic-clad mind of a trained engineer, the faith of a spreadsheet fundamentalist. At that early date, he understood that the Internet was going to remake the world. It was an insight that didn't strike most of his elders on Wall Street as very likely, though his own hedge fund was keen to invest in Web sites. Bezos and his boss, an eccentric computer scientist called David Shaw, even kicked around the idea of creating an "everything store"—a site that would serve as the mother of all intermediaries between the world's manufacturers and its customers.

But Bezos methodically studied the possibilities for commerce on the burgeoning medium, and considered that big idea a few steps early. Before consumers would shop at an everything store, they needed to acclimate to online shopping. He went searching for the ideal gateway product. The key would be to find a business that could easily be mastered by a small, underfunded operation—that would quickly build the trust of consumers, that didn't require traveling the world to source inventory, that would allow for low-cost experimentation. After meticulous analysis, he decided that books—not office supplies, not music, not socks— were his best play. After all, you never returned a book for being ill fitting, and books were sturdy enough to order without anxiety about their getting crushed or jostled in transit. Bezos quit his job, packed his Upper West Side apartment, drove to Seattle, and started the firm he would eventually name Amazon.

The allure and power of the Internet are due to its infinitude. More than any physical space, it is all-inclusive, inexhaustibly capacious. Bezos intuited this, too. He called his new company the "Earth's Largest Bookstore." And in that description, there was the essence of the everything store. At first, this was a powerful ruse. Amazon didn't have shelves or warehouses, just a relationship with the big distributors. This was the first of thousands of smart choices that made Bezos's initial empty promise of gargantuan size into a self-fulfilling prophecy.

JEFF BEZOS HAD ARRIVED at a core truth: The world stood on the cusp of a knowledge boom, a nuclear explosion of information that would remake economies. Indeed, this is what the Internet (and Bezos) has brought to pass. Knowledge has never been more abundant, never more central to the creation of wealth. Bezos even had a vision, however underdeveloped, that this revolution would birth a new style of firm: the knowledge monopoly.[*]

There have been various stabs at coining a term to capture the dominant role of Google, Amazon, Facebook, and Apple. Mark Zuckerberg has called his company a "utility," perhaps un-

---

[*] Economists and antitrust lawyers won't care for my casual use of the term "monopoly." It has a technical meaning, they will grump. "Oligopoly" might be a more accurate description of some of the markets I describe. These criticisms are fair, except I'm not making a technical argument. Indeed, I believe that technical arguments have strangled the discussion. My hope is that we revive "monopoly" as a core piece of political rhetoric that broadly denotes dominant firms with pernicious powers. This might not fly in the bar association, but such usage has a proud and productive lineage tracing back to Thomas Jefferson.

aware how the term is historically an invitation for invasive regulation. But there's something to his suggestion. In the industrial age, utilities were infrastructure that the public deemed essential to the functioning of everyday life—electricity and gas, water and sewage. In the end, the country couldn't function without them, and the government removed these companies from the vicissitudes of the market, leashing them to publicly appointed commissions that set their prices.

In the knowledge economy, the essential pieces of infrastructure are intellectual. With the inexhaustible choice made possible by the Internet comes a new imperative—the need for new tools capable of navigating the vastness. The world's digital trove of knowledge isn't terribly useful without mechanisms for searching and sorting the ethereal holdings. That's the trick Amazon—and the other knowledge monopolists—have managed. Amazon didn't just create the world's biggest bookstore; it made its store far more usable, far more efficient, than browsing the aisles of a Barnes and Noble or cruising a library's card catalog. And beyond that, Amazon anticipated your desires, using its storehouse of data to recommend your next purchase, to strongly suggest a course for navigating knowledge.

This is the strange essence of the new knowledge monopolies. They don't actually produce knowledge; they just sift and organize it.* We rely on a small handful of companies to provide us with a sense of hierarchy, to identify what we should read and what we should ignore, to pick informational winners and losers. It's incredible economic and cultural power that they have

---

*Amazon does publish books, mostly mass-market genre fiction. It also experimented with publishing Kindle Singles, which included serious long-form journalism, a project it has since dialed back.

amassed because of a sudden change in the strange economics of the commodity they traffic in, a change they hastened.

ADAM SMITH, it's fair to say, didn't anticipate Jeff Bezos. When the Scotsman first sketched the workings of capitalism, he had plenty to say about land, labor, and capital. Those were the fundamental elements of markets, and they became the bedrock concepts of mainstream economics. Knowledge never entered deeply into Smith's thinking about trade. And for nearly two hundred years, the discipline of economics barely entertained the possibility that knowledge might really be the necessary ingredient for growth.

But Jeff Bezos was born into a world obsessed with knowledge. After World War II, the American elite began to define itself on the basis of its brains, not the happenstance of its daddies. That's why Ivy League universities came to require standardized tests as the basis for admissions. Those universities, once finishing schools for the rich, fully remade themselves as "knowledge factories," in the words of the University of California's midcentury chancellor, Clark Kerr. The government considered research—the production of knowledge—a worthy recipient for massive infusions of cash. Washington poured money into science and social science, practical engineering and wonderfully impractical theorizing alike.

Economics might not have had much to say about knowledge, but knowledge was dictating the trajectory of the late-twentieth-century economy. The sources of growth were increasingly intangible—the manipulation of symbols, the collection and exploitation of data, the invention of formulas and theories. Put differently, wealth was more likely to be hatched from computer code, a television series, a patent, a financial instrument. King Knowledge even determined the fruit of the soil. Take Monsanto, which produces the seeds that account for 80 percent of all corn and 90 percent of all soybeans grown in the United States. What Monsanto possesses, what it ferociously hoards, is the genetic traits of these seeds. Its comparative advantage isn't factories, but laboratories.

Of course, economists could plainly see what was happening, but they didn't quite know what to make of the change, at least not at first. Knowledge was a flummoxing thing to the dismal scientists. It was different from all other goods. People paid for cars and buildings because those goods were scarce. Or they had a quality that Paul Romer, the economist who has thought hardest about knowledge, called "rivalry"—if I own a shovel, you can't own that shovel, too. Such rivalry can never be the case for knowledge. Yes, it takes a lot of money to engineer a new seed or to fund a lengthy work of investigative journalism. But once the recipe is complete and the article is published, it can be copied for free, or nearly free.

If left to the devices of the market, the price of knowledge would quickly collapse, destroyed by the ease with which it could be freely copied. But the government doesn't permit this collapse. One of its primary economic responsibilities is preserving the value of knowledge. It shelters the creators of knowledge from the rigors of the competitive marketplace, granting them a temporary state-sponsored monopoly in the form of patents and copyrights. Intellectual property is an ancient tradition, so venerable that James Madison pushed for its enshrinement in Article I, Section 8, of the U.S. Constitution. This canon of law is meant to balance two inimical concerns. On the one hand, it creates conditions that foster creativity and innovation. Who would pour her life into a creation if some knockoff artist could get rich off an effortless facsimile? On the other hand, the law eventually phases out the monopolies (although Disney manages to keep extending the terms of copyright law to keep Mickey Mouse under its tightest control). Knowledge is too important to remain the eternal possession of any company or individual. We know that future achievements must build on past ones; that monopolies, over the long run, drain the creativity from an economy.

This system worked well enough over the years, despite the overly aggressive defenses that Hollywood and the music industry often mounted to protect the sanctity of their possessions. But modernity also posed a challenge to these protections. Long before the Internet, copying had slowly implanted itself as a fact of modern life. Generations that can recall analog existence will note that VCRs, Xerox machines, and cassette tapes made mimesis an everyday thing. Still, those technologies were limited. Duplicating a movie or curating a mixtape entailed time, hassle, expense.

With the Internet, those impediments disappeared entirely. Any college kid with bandwidth could download more or less every song in recorded history, without spending a penny. And even that example understates the full ramifications of new technologies. Cory Doctorow, an early pioneer of the cyber-frontier, has fairly described the condition this way: "We can't stop copying on the Internet, because the Internet is a copying machine. Literally. There is no way to communicate on the Internet without sending copies. You might think you're 'loading' a web page, but what's really happening is that a copy is being placed on your computer, which then displays it in your browser."

It didn't take long for the implications of this to terrify the entertainment industry. Panic washed over the music moguls, as Napster, Grokster, and other newfangled sites smashed their business to pieces. The recording behemoths blindly sued whoever they could. (Absurd lawsuit: George Clinton, of Parliament-Funkadelic fame, was sued for sampling himself.) This torrent of litigation seemed ominous at the time, the beginning of a chilly new age of control. But, in the end, it was a hopeless defense of a doomed model.

The culture had changed. Once an underground, amateur pastime, the bootlegging of intellectual property became an accepted business practice. Sites like the *Huffington Post* liberally plucked the best paragraphs of news stories, with a grudging link back to the original item. Google scanned every book it could find. Apple's advertisements preached, "Rip, Mix, Burn—After all, it's your music." Larry Lessig, a law professor who served as a chief champion of this new era, declared: "The defining feature of the Internet is that it leaves resources free."

We could portray the changes as a matter of piracy—and there was surely a lot of that. But that wasn't the significant development. Media accepted the economic collapse of knowledge, as if it were as irresistible as the weather. Newspapers and magazines remade their business strategies to accommodate change. Since the birth of newspapers and magazines, publishers had recovered their costs by charging readers to buy their creations. Even if the purchase price didn't cover the costs of reporting and publishing, it was a major source of revenue and crucial to advertisers. Madison Avenue regarded a paying subscriber as an engaged reader worth the effort to reach. But that thinking didn't mesh with the Internet. Stewart Brand famously issued the nostrum "Information wants to be free." To charge for information was to walk away from a historic business opportunity. The Internet gifted media with unprecedented scale. It was a superhighway to a world of readers that would never dump a quarter into a newspaper box, let alone pay the hefty charge for home delivery. No direct mail campaign, no television advertising, could equal the marketing potential of the Internet. "Value is derived from plentitude [*sic*]," *Wired* editor Kevin Kelly counseled, advice that was adopted on the widest scale.

This was a conscious change, but newspapers hadn't entirely understood how they were abandoning an old tenet of their business. Media had long followed a venerable strategy that suggested that profit could be found in the bundling of products—the way Microsoft Office jammed consumers into buying Excel with Word, though they may not have had any need for a spreadsheet. That's what newspapers and magazines were: bundles of articles. For print, the strategy worked well enough. Readers might want only the *Washington Post* sports section, but they couldn't buy that alone, so they paid a heftier fee for foreign coverage, local news, and the rest of the obligatory package. But with the advent of Web pages, the bundle vanished as a strategy. Online newspapers and magazines ceased to exist primarily as an anthology of articles. There were no subscriptions to buy; and readers quickly habituated to jumping from site to site, link to link. Pieces came to exist as their own untethered entities—back when she was with Google, Marissa Mayer called them the "atomic unit of consumption for news," flourishing or sinking on their own. "Each individual article," Mayer said, "should be self-sustaining."

This was, on the surface, a boon for knowledge. Never before had it been possible to learn so much, to acquire such valuable material, and at no cost. Such exponential growth couldn't be captured with statistical precision. But there were suggestive numbers. By the year 2002, our digital storehouse of knowledge was suddenly larger than humanity's analog cache. And that was just the Internet's infancy. Between 2006 and 2012, the world's information output grew tenfold. Serious analysts, without a hint of hyperbole, compared it to the emergence from the Dark Ages.

This abundance of free material, however, created a new form of scarcity—with so much to read, see, and hear, with the unending web of links, it became almost impossible to grab an audience's attention. David Foster Wallace called the condition Total Noise. With it, our reading became peripatetic, less focused. Back in the seventies, Herbert Simon, the Nobel-winning economist, took these inchoate sentiments and explained them rigorously: "What information consumes is rather obvious. It consumes the attention of its recipients. Hence a wealth of information creates a poverty of attention." The poverty of attention, the inability to hold a reader's attention for sustained time, that's the crucial concept. It's an existential problem for producers of knowledge—and a source of strain and confusion for consumers of it. Navigating the vastness of the Internet can feel like getting marooned in the middle of the ocean, both terrifying and sublime in its overwhelmingness.

This condition has grievously wounded old media, which has spent more than a decade searching for a plausible strategy to regrip its audience, a war on the poverty of attention. But the very factors that squeeze these companies—the wealth of knowledge, the scarcity of attention—have fueled the rise of the new informational monopolies. These companies take the massive, ever-growing blob of knowledge and impose order on it. Amazon organizes retail into a coherent, usable marketplace, to make no mention of it being the largest, most trafficked bookstore in human history; Google culls the entirety of the Web so that we have some sensible progression for considering its offerings; Facebook provides a directory of people, as well as a method for managing social lives. Without these tools, the Internet becomes unusable. "Searching and filtering are all that stand between this world and the Library of Babel," the science writer James Gleick has argued.

THE BIG TECH COMPANIES didn't just benefit from the economic collapse of knowledge. They maneuvered to shred the value of knowledge, so that old media would come to helplessly depend on their platforms. There was a precedent for this strategy. When Apple created the iPod, it created a device with the capacity to hold thousands of digitized songs—ideal for amassing pirated music, which was flowing freely at that moment. Steve Jobs could have easily designed the iPod to make it inhospitable to stolen music. But he initially refused to build the iPod so that it would block unlicensed content. At the same time Jobs's device enabled piracy, Jobs himself decried digital thievery. He was playing a cunning game: After helping push the music business to the brink, he would save it and come to dominate it. Eighteen months after creating the iPod, he debuted an online store, iTunes, that became the place where a vast percentage of all music was purchased. In the face of piracy, enfeebled producers lay prostrate in front of their new savior, even if Apple dismembered the once profitable album by selling individual songs for ninety-nine cents. From the wreckage Apple helped create, it built a new monopoly—60 percent of digital downloaded music is sold through iTunes—although streaming services have begun to weaken its decade-long grip on the business.

It's sometimes hard to grasp the pecuniary motives of the big tech companies, because they strike such an idealistic pose. There's no doubt that they believe in their own righteousness, but they also practice corporate gamesmanship, with all the established tricks: lobbying, purchasing support in think tanks and universities, quietly donating money to advocacy groups that promote their interests. The journalist Robert Levine has written, "Google has as much interest in free online media as General Motors does in cheap gasoline. That's why the company spends millions of dollars lobbying to weaken copyright." Google and Facebook penalize companies that don't share their vision of intellectual property. When newspapers and magazines require subscriptions to access their pieces, Google and Facebook tend to bury them; articles protected by stringent paywalls almost never have the popularity that algorithms reward with prominence. Google, according to documents that have surfaced in lawsuits against the company, is blunt about using its power to bend the media business to its model. Jonathan Rosenberg, the vice president of product management, told company brass in 2006 that Google must "pressure premium content providers to change their model to free." It's a perfectly rational stance. The big tech companies become far more valuable if they serve as a gateway to free knowledge, if they provide a portal to an open and comprehensive collection of material.

Amazon doesn't quite preach the same gospel, but it shares

the same basic approach. It deflated the price of the books that it sells and made implicit arguments about their value. By unilaterally setting the price of the e-book at $9.99, far lower than paper, Bezos falsely implied that the cost of producing a book resided in printing and shipping, not in intellectual capital, creativity, and years of effort. Bezos implicitly argued that technology would continue to drive prices lower over time, an argument that had the effect of making his opponents in book publishing that resisted such deflationary pressures look like greedy enemies of the reader. In truth, revenue from books was of secondary concern to Bezos. The profit margin on each copy of Zadie Smith or Robert Caro it sells hardly matters in the scheme of things. What counts is addicting readers to its devices and site, so that Amazon becomes a central fixture in their lives, an epicenter of leisure and consumption—exactly the same aspiration that Google and Facebook harbor.

They are getting ever closer to that goal. Amazon, Google, and Facebook are now the primary bundlers of articles, books, and video. They are the ones that create a usable, coherent product from its disparate parts. Their business model is infinitely better than the one it displaced. Google and Facebook don't pay for any of the articles that they present to the consumer, and their scale of offerings is infinitely larger than anything the old media companies could ever muster. They are, after all, organizing the entire output of humanity.

Of course, this is not an innocent activity—even though the tech companies disavow any responsibility for the material they publish and promote. They plead that they are mere platforms, neutral utilities for everyone's use and everyone's benefit. When Facebook was assailed for abetting the onslaught of false news stories during the 2016 presidential campaign—a steady stream of fabricated right-wing conspiracies that boosted Donald Trump's candidacy—Mark Zuckerberg initially disclaimed any culpability. "Our goal is to give every person a voice," he posted on Facebook, washing his hands of the matter. It's galling to watch Zuckerberg walk away from the catastrophic collapse of the news business and the degradation of American civic culture, because his site has played such a seminal role in both. Though Zuckerberg denies it, the process of guiding the public to information is a source of tremendous cultural and political power. In the olden days, we described that power as gatekeeping—and it was a sacred obligation.

Five

KEEPERS OF THE BIG
GATE IN THE SKY

LIKE DONALD TRUMP, Silicon Valley is part of the great American tradition of sham populism. With not quite the same furor as our current president, Silicon Valley came to power on the basis of its anti-elitism. It presented itself an antidote to the old Acela Corridor establishment, which it accused of condescending to the masses and zealously guarding its own prerogatives at everyone else's expense. Facebook was hailed as a mechanism that would help diminish the importance of clubbable gasbag pundits; Amazon would bust up the cartel of effete New York book publishers. This critique was not purely an exercise in denunciation. It was coupled with an alternative vision of society, a vision of amateurs producing knowledge for the joy of it, a faith in the wisdom of crowds. Silicon Valley views its role in history as that of the disruptive agent that shatters the grip of the sclerotic, self-perpetuating mediocrity that constitutes the American elite.

On the surface, the tech companies seem aware of the danger that they might repeat the sins of the very cohort they critique. After Silicon Valley supplies its users with tools to make decisions for themselves, it claims to step out of the way and recede unassumingly. This ostentatious humility serves an important purpose. It obscures the nature of its power. Silicon Valley routinely trashes cultural and economic gatekeepers—while its own companies are the most imposing gatekeepers in human history.

Jeff Bezos is the most populist of the tech CEOs, and the most strident critic of gatekeepers among them. But his sniping at the old elite apparently masks a more complicated set of emotions and desires, his own unreconciled attraction to the object of his disdain.

IN THE SUMMER OF 2013, Bezos bought the *Washington Post*. The transaction came as a shock to the elite system. For eight decades, the newspaper had been run by the Graham family—a clan that came to represent the noblest, most public-minded strain of American aristocracy, or at least that was their reputation in their own crust of society. Bezos seemed a strange successor to mount the old pillar of the *Post*. For starters, he came from what he called, with some self-satisfaction, the "other Washington." The distance he described was more than geographic. Politics and policy, the sources of the *Post*'s cachet, never seemed to hold his attention for very long. Whereas doyennes and pundits still regarded the ownership of the *Post* as an enviable trophy, Bezos posed as the opposite sort of guy: a man who regarded devoted institutionalism as lazy, timid, and self-destructive. But here he was buying a venerable institution, a cultural icon that spelled its name in a Gothic font and reveled in its swashbuckling past.

The sale wasn't seen as just a transition in ownership regimes; it was a dying elite handing over power to an ascendant one. Don Graham, the chief executive of the *Washington Post*, admitted that he simply couldn't find a way forward into the glorious digital future. Although he had never imagined selling the company, he had no choice. "Seven years of declining revenues will give you new ideas," he told one interviewer. Instead of flailing along, painfully maintaining the illusion that his family might devise an innovative plan to salvage its fortunes, he was turning to a technology mogul for a bailout.

When Graham announced the surrender of his heirloom, Bezos was nowhere to be seen in the building. He remained at a continental remove, merely sending a warm email to his new staff. It would be several weeks before he appeared in the newsroom that he now bankrolled. To be fair, the *Post* was hardly a grand purchase by his standards. The paper cost about $250 million, a snack not a meal for a man then worth $25 billion.

All the ways in which Graham and Bezos hailed from different places with different values were irrepressibly displayed, like plumage. But what observers missed was that Bezos had actively and carefully studied for his new role. Sure, he was a technologist and retailer, not a newsman. But, like Graham, he was an informational gatekeeper—a figure who stood between consumers and the knowledge they craved. It's just that you would never think of Graham and Bezos as representatives of the same tribe, they went about their jobs so differently. And in that difference, we can see the perils of Bezos and his view of the world.

"GATEKEEPING," AS A TERM APPLIED to media, entered the vernacular in the aftermath of World War II. After witnessing great cultures enthusiastically submit to fascism, American social scientists began to scour their own society for weaknesses. How did public opinion work in this country? What fascist tendencies were lurking on the crabgrass frontier? A rash of academic studies attempted to discern how information traveled to the common man, probing for points that demagogues might exploit. In the era—just before Edward R. Murrow and Walter Cronkite came to represent journalistic authority—newspapers were the nation's information byway. They, therefore, were essential subjects for vigorous study.

In a medieval village, the gatekeeper had the power to admit (or turn away) entrants into the communal sanctum. At a newspaper, it was the editor who played this part. That was the insight of a Boston University professor called David Manning White. In 1950, he published a charmingly simple and methodologically dodgy study of that function. None of the defects in his work prevented it from standing as a landmark in the emerging field of media studies.

White had struck up a correspondence with an editor at a small newspaper. Reporting on his findings, White hid his subject behind a pseudonym, Mr. Gates. For a week, Mr. Gates took careful notes on the wire stories he chose to reprint and those he ignored. He turned over these logs to White, who read them carefully for clues to the subconscious impulses guiding Mr. Gates's choices. The raw material provided a crystalline view of one low-level gatekeeper's mind, and from there the professor made the most of his data. White concluded that the newspaper was a product of Mr. Gates's biases—his preference for narrative over statistics, his professional caution.

That's a quaint thesis, the idea that certain well-placed individuals, full of conscious and submerged biases, exert control over the flow of information. But it's also the truth. Some information comes to the fore, some of it recedes. Gatekeepers make those calls. Even if they self-consciously never quite consider their power, gatekeepers must believe that they know what their audience wants, and they must believe they know what's best for their audience.

At newspapers, the trade-offs were clear enough. A front page can highlight only so many stories, and certain positions on the front page connote greater import than others. Besides, long before stories percolate to publication, editors make the even more elemental choice of how to assign limited reportorial resources. Not knowing where their work will lead, they must make a judgment about its potential worth. Walter Lippmann, who wrote one of the first great works of media criticism in 1920, warned about the dangers inherent in this task: "So long as there is interposed between the ordinary citizen and the facts a news organization determining by entirely private and unexamined standards, no matter how lofty, what he shall know, and hence what he shall believe, no one will be able to say that the substance of democratic government is secure."

It's easy to romanticize the *Washington Post* as the counter-example that disproves Lippmann's warning—especially because Hollywood has already guided us to a heroic and glamorous narrative, casting Robert Redford as the paper's signature scribe. Under the stewardship of the Graham family—which took hold of the paper in 1933 in a bankruptcy auction—the *Post* eventually became a serious organ of reportage. Don Graham's grandfather, Eugene Meyer, spoke of his new duties with solemn obligation:

> The newspaper's duty is to its readers and to the public at large and not to private interests of its owners. In the pursuit of truth, the newspaper shall be prepared to make sacrifices of its material fortunes, if such a course be necessary for the public good. The newspaper shall not be the ally of any special interest, but shall be fair and free and wholesome in its outlook on public affairs and public men.

Meyer—and his son-in-law Philip Graham—could afford to speak of their mission in such high-minded language. The family lost $1 million a year for the first twenty years that it held the paper. But after the *Post* merged with its crosstown rival, the *Washington Times-Herald,* it gained one of the country's firmest media monopolies. By 1964, nearly half of metropolitan Washington took the *Post* at home. Its Sunday circulation peaked at 1.2 million. Like the Sulzbergers, the Graham family preached an ideal of "disinterestedness," an ethos that demanded they rise above the biases of their social class. This was a quasi-religious code. As the political analyst John B. Judis has written about that defining generation of newspaper ownership, "News was to be separate from editorial judgment, and editorial judgment, while favoring distinct policy alternatives, was to be free of partisan attachments."

In its most noble moments, the *Washington Post* took down power, even as it cozied up to it. Phil's widow and successor, Katharine, sipped terrapin soup with Henry Kissinger, at the same time her paper shredded his lies about Vietnam. She frequently found herself standing her ground in the face of presidents, who pleaded with her to silence her reporters in the name of national security. Nixon's scabrous attorney general, John Mitchell, once famously threatened Carl Bernstein about the risks of running a forthcoming exposé: "Katie Graham's gonna get her tit caught in a big fat wringer if that's published." To Mitchell's eternal humiliation, the *Post* ran the story in spite of his bluster and printed a mammary-free version of his vulgar warning. After Nixon's downfall, Graham would occasionally wear a necklace with a golden breast.

That sort of courage in the face of power makes a journalist's pulse quicken, but it also contains the potential for abuse. Any organization that can take down a president is worth staring at with awe, but also fear. Look at the alleged machinations of Rupert Murdoch's papers in London, acting on implicit deals that their owner reportedly cuts with politicians. It requires no imagination to see how less-than-fastidious media owners could wage a self-interested, self-aggrandizing campaign through their outlets.

Phil Graham, it could be argued, abused the *Post* in this way. He was a serial kingmaker and used his paper to further the backroom shenanigans that gave him such pleasure. As David Halberstam wrote, Graham "hated for the *Post* or its writers to look as though they were not on the inside and connected." In 1952, he threw his paper behind Dwight Eisenhower's presidential bid, so much so that he suppressed the work of the cartoonist Herblock, who didn't like Ike, during the final two weeks of the campaign. It was Lyndon Johnson who later ignited Graham's imagination. The newspaper magnate even helped write the speech in which the Senate majority leader announced his presidential ambitions.

And slightly more debasing than that, Graham would find himself on his hands and knees searching for a contact lens that popped out of LBJ's eye, moments before he delivered the address. This coziness helps account for the *Post*'s editorial support of Vietnam through 1969. (Johnson appointed the paper's executive editor Russ Wiggins ambassador to the United Nations, as a reward for his loyal shilling for the war.) The fact that the paper would eventually turn hard against the war, and would publish important critical reportage, hardly erases this fact.

But lofty ideals were transmitted from one generation of Grahams to the next. Before Don Graham could assume his birthright, he needed to intimately learn his city and its paper. He worked as a cop in the Ninth Precinct and as a sports editor, an apprenticeship in humility. The Grahams, to their credit, eventually acknowledged that their power required restraints beyond their own best intentions. A code of behavior governed the *Post*, as it did most major metropolitan dailies. It culminated in near-daily issuances of mea culpas, published on the inside of the paper in the form of corrections. An ombudsman was installed to issue weekly evaluations of the *Post*'s adherence to its ideals. The business side of the paper was constitutionally cordoned from the rest of the operation—the separation of church and state was the metaphor used to describe the organization's power structure and the inviolability of editorial prerogatives. Some of this was a matter of newspaper convention, and it often failed to prevent terrible lapses, but it also signaled devotion to the high calling of gatekeeping.

DON GRAHAM'S SUCCESSOR DOESN'T think of himself as a gatekeeper. Indeed, he would abhor having that moniker slapped on his innovative name. He considers the species an enemy of progress. In his view, gatekeepers are the protectors of the timid status quo. They quash breakthrough ideas. A letter Bezos once wrote to Amazon investors could also be read as a manifesto—and as a broadside against the likes of Don Graham. He thundered, "Even well-meaning gatekeepers slow innovation."

This isn't simply a slogan, it is a highly developed theory of history. The narrative goes like this: Once upon a time, the world needed gatekeepers. Resources were limited, so they had to be prudently rationed by enlightened elites. Scarcity, however, has now faded into the past thanks to the collapsing price of computing. This was a revolution in the means of production. Cheaply and easily, anyone could publish a book, broadcast an opinion, launch a company, create a Web site. Bureaucracies and clunky corporations continue to ploddingly exist. But really, who needs them? One by one, they have begun to suffer and fade. "I see the elimination of gatekeepers everywhere," Bezos said.

Amazon, of course, is meant to be the antithesis of these antique organizations. Bezos sees his company as a platform—the world's greatest bazaar, where anybody can sell their wares and anybody can buy them. No gatekeepers lurk in his domain, waiting to capriciously trample dreams. "The most radical and transformative of inventions are often those that empower others to unleash their creativity," he has written. It's this sentiment that informs his disdain for book publishing. In the olden days, big houses in New York impeded creativity—editing, printing, distributing a handful of volumes each year. If a writer somehow failed to catch the fancy of a New York publisher, she was consigned to irrelevance. Amazon disrupted the hell out of that arrangement. Anyone with a novel in a desk drawer could publish directly to Amazon. It was almost as easy as posting to Facebook. Unlike the New York snobs, Amazon didn't impose any dictates, didn't demand revisions or ask questions of an author's visions. Without the bloated Manhattan middlemen—and their expense accounts and latte-fetching minions—writers could take home a larger swath of revenue. This, in Bezos's telling, was an unabashed triumph of democracy, "Take a look at the Kindle bestseller list, and compare it to the *New York Times* best-seller list—which is more diverse?" The Kindle list was certainly more populist—filled with mechanistic romance novels and stilted science fiction, published by writers who pump out books at a pace that allows little time for thinking, eating, or sleep.

This was, indeed, a radically different approach to the stewardship of knowledge. Gatekeepers like Graham had styled themselves as leaders, as a privileged and enlightened elite. They had obligations to their communities; they thought hard about profits, but also about the dangers of rampant commercialism. Bezos views his business—and even the *Washington Post*—differently. As a matter of principle, he doesn't pose as a guardian of the community and a custodian of high ideals. That would just muzzle the market, preventing it from communicating its wishes. He believes in letting consumers, the customers around whom the world spins, have the final word. When he took over the *Post*, he flashed a hint of this thinking. "Our touchstone will be readers, understanding what they care about—government, local leaders, restaurant openings, scout troops, businesses, charities, governors, sports—and working backwards from there."

An obvious falsehood resides at the heart of Bezos's account. He may have no wish to play the role of gatekeeper, but that's exactly what he is. Yes, the old mode of gatekeeping excluded books from shelves and articles from magazines. Amazon, by contrast, sells nearly every cultural artifact produced by Western civilization. But let's not confuse Amazon with a utopian experiment in participatory democracy. Amazon always gives better treatment to some artifacts than others—promoting them in email, on its home page, and through its recommendation algorithms. This is tremendous cultural power, especially given how so many of Amazon's competitors have melted in the face of its size and prowess.

Amazon doesn't necessarily want to own whole industries, but it likes to control them. With publishing, Amazon has become the indispensable store. It sells 65 percent of all e-books and over 40 percent of all books. Publishing depends on Amazon for its health—an awkward, vulnerable position. At the same time publishers rely on Amazon, Amazon would like to destroy publishers, or at least severely curtail their influence. Amazon is both publishing's primary outlet and its primary competition.

JEFF BEZOS HAS FAMOUSLY MANAGED to convince Wall Street that his retail operation doesn't require short-term profits; that quarterly earnings are nothing, compared with the riches over the horizon that will arrive once Amazon cements its dominance. With such forbearance, he can afford to experiment, to probe publishing for points of weakness. Not all of Amazon's many efforts to seize terrain from the publishers have worked. In 2011, Amazon set up an old-fashioned New York publishing house. It hired eminent editors, installed them in a high-rent office, and gave them a pile of money to acquire books. That business floundered when it paid large advances to buy celebrity memoirs (Penny Marshall,

Billy Ray Cyrus) and literary fiction that flopped, even with all of the company's might behind the effort.

But that was a conventional effort, and Amazon is not a conventional company. It has succeeded by creating a new set of rules. Rather than working with established authors, it cultivates new ones. Or rather, it has built its own mass-market imprints, recruiting an army of genre writers, and it has encouraged frustrated lawyers and fed-up schoolteachers to self-publish their novels directly to the Kindle. Many of these writers have folders full of rejection letters that they have received from New York publishers. They are willing, for the most part, to work without receiving advance payments. So, Amazon incurs little or no financial risk in backing their work. It finds an audience for its writers by pricing their books very low, or even giving them away for free. An unknown thriller writer, after all, can hope to compete with Stephen King only by selling novels at a fraction of the price. This meshes perfectly with Amazon's preferred method: the sale of cheap goods, with profit reaped through high volume.

Amazon wanted to bend the entirety of the book-publishing industry to match its own reification of low prices. It has tried to impose this ethos on traditional publishers, too. When Bezos debuted the Kindle, he surprised publishers by announcing that Amazon would sell e-books for $9.99—a sum that Bezos arbitrarily plucked and then blared to the public without giving the publishers any warning. This was brilliant gamesmanship. Bezos cemented a public impression about the value of e-books. There was a nefarious assumption buried in his argument: that the price of a book could be ascribed to material costs, not to the writing and editing. Bezos simply couldn't find any economic value in intellectual capital, creativity, and the time required for complex thought.

If Bezos views himself as the vanguard of change, publishers see themselves as the resistance to it. They cling to the belief that they are in an artisanal line of work—practicing a craft that demands hard-earned experience and a painstaking process of revision. We know this is not always the case—maybe not often the case—but there are implications to this view. The foundational assumption of book publishing holds that writing isn't a simple task, and that writers lack the cognitive ability to see the flaws in their own work; writers need a guiding hand. A book can manage its way through the marketplace only with expertise (in marketing, publicity, distribution) that the writer doesn't possess. Amazon, on the other hand, considers the profession to be filled with "antediluvian losers," as one of the company's early employees described its attitude toward traditional book publishers.

Amazon's negotiating tactics with publishers are almost sadistic. The smaller the publisher, the more extravagant the pressure to comply with Amazon's wishes. University presses watch as their e-books fade from view, as Amazon negotiates even more favorable terms for itself. At one point, the company lumped its contracts with small publishers under an initiative called the Gazelle Project, a label conceived after Bezos quipped that his team "should approach these small publishers the way a cheetah would pursue a sickly gazelle." Amazon has been only a fraction more genteel in dealing with the larger publishing houses. When sparring over terms with the publishing conglomerate Macmillan, it stripped the company's books of the buttons that allow consumers to purchase them. In its dealings with Hachette, it delayed shipment of books. When cutting a deal with publishers, it doesn't bother with innuendo. According to some who have sat across the table from Amazon, the company leaves no doubt that it will suppress a publisher's performance in its algorithms and eliminate its books from its emails if the company rejects its terms.

We can describe this as good business, but Amazon is coy about its cultural power. It's gatekeeping on a scale that Don Graham and his ilk never imagined. Amazon doesn't just have the power to bring books to the public's attention, or to deny knowledge to an audience. It wants to radically remake the production of culture. In his most boastful moments Bezos will admit his revolutionary ambitions: "No technology, not even one as elegant as the book, lasts forever."

SOON AFTER JEFF BEZOS BOUGHT the *Washington Post*, he issued a dictate: The paper could hire lots of writers, designers, and engineers, but not editors. He didn't believe in editing, a prejudice he likely imported from his war on book publishing—a view he eventually softened. (Bezos also suggested that the paper experiment with dropping vowels from its stories, according to a report in *New York* magazine.)

We're in the early days of the Jeff Bezos era of ownership, and it's too early to make any judgments about the experiment. There's a widespread perception that the paper has vastly improved itself under his leadership. Bezos has kept the paper in the hands of Marty Baron, a legendary scoop hound with a resolute faith in the methodologies of old-fashioned journalism. The paper has deepened its commitment to covering politics and published painstaking investigations. At the same time, Bezos has shown a commitment to turning the *Washington Post* into an Amazon company. The paper has grown its Web traffic by leaps and bounds, growth fueled, in part, by disposable pieces that are engineered to appeal to the widest audience, written with sensationalist headlines, often making bombastic points. Perhaps both visions of journalism can coexist, with the schlock subsidizing the excellent stuff.

Even if Bezos saves the paper, we shouldn't applaud too loudly. The population of informational oligarchs shrinks a little more every year. Once upon a time, Washington had four daily newspapers. By the Reagan administration, it came to have the *Post*, trailed only by a little-read right-wing organ. And that condition was itself unusually bountiful. "By the early twenty-first century, literally 99.9 percent of contemporary daily papers are a monopoly in their own cities," the media critic Ben Bagdikian once tabulated. Since he did the math, a depressingly large percentage of those broadsheets have perished. Back in the eighties, a convention of the most powerful media magnates in the country would have filled a small ballroom—local oligarchs would have mingled with national ones. Then, by the late nineties, a wave of consolidation shrank that group to a size that could fit around a conference table.

Over the first decades of consolidation, the new corporate ideal came to resemble Time Warner, with its portfolio of magazines, record labels, cable news networks, movie studios, premium movie channels, a book publisher, and a cable company, not to mention its ill-fated merger with AOL. Entertainment is a big business, but also an unpredictable one. Success hinged on generating the likes of *Harry Potter* or *Batman*, big-budget smashes and marketing bonanzas. These triumphs were hard to manufacture on a regular basis, and the studios had to account for the inevitable *Ishtar*s. So, moguls sought to hedge. For a media company to survive the inevitable stinkers, it will try to distribute its risky investments across a broad array of steadier businesses that live in the same entertainment neighborhood, with the distant promise of synergy.

The consolidation of media also stemmed from government loosening its regulatory guard. There were limits to how much local power the Graham family could amass, at least until the George W. Bush administration. Before Republicans remade the rules, the FCC prohibited newspaper owners from acquiring a television station in the same market, and vice versa. This was the broad thrust of federal policy: When a merger looked to reduce the number of media outlets, no matter how marginally, the impulse was to reject it. Regulators and judges chanted the phrase "diversity of voices." The Supreme Court viewed the First Amendment as reason enough for the government to block media companies (especially broadcasters) from becoming monopolists. As Justice Byron White put it in 1969, "It is the right of the viewers and listeners, not the right of broadcasters, which is paramount." To protect these rights, the government forced Rupert Murdoch to sell the *Boston Herald* in 1994 before it would allow him to buy back the Fox affiliate in town. And it blocked the Graham family rival, Joe Allbritton, from owning both the *Washington Star* and a local television affiliate.

We shouldn't pretend that these rules were impenetrable bulwarks. They were riddled with loopholes that permitted the likes of the Tribune Company to dominate Chicago. But there's no doubting that the government caused empire-builders to think twice before embarking on media spending sprees. The government even paid careful attention to the tweedy book publishers. When Random House bought Alfred A. Knopf in 1960, Dwight Eisenhower's attorney general, William Rogers, was alarmed enough to have his office make calls about the implications of the deal. (He let the matter drop when he learned that the new entity would control less than 1 percent of the market.) When Time-Life, the blue whale of publishing, wanted to inhale Random House a few years later, it ultimately backed away from the deal after the Justice Department professed its displeasure with the idea.

By the beginning of the century, all those curbs, however, had faded. No matter the party in power, the perils of media bigness no longer caused government much bother. While the regulators placed their shackles in storage, technology created the possibility of a whole new species of giants, bigger than humanity had ever encountered. Once upon a time, media moved through the world in rivers that never connected—radio signals had nothing to do with the mail, which had nothing to do with movie houses. But with the Internet, all media came rushing down the same digital falls. The computer screen began to simultaneously take the place of the post office, the television set, the stereo, and the newspaper. During the nineties, this was called convergence, and it was correctly touted as a gold mine.

Taking advantage of this opportunity required a different sort of thinking and corporate organization. Conglomerates could never truly create a meaningful whole from their array of publishing imprints, magazines, and movie studios. That's why a behemoth like Time Warner looked scary, but never did dominate the way its opponents feared or its investors hoped. At best, the conglomerates were a collection of powerful, profitable fiefdoms, reporting back to a mother ship in Manhattan. Sometimes, they even worked in the same skyscraper. The promised synergies, however, amounted to nothing more than a catchy slogan.

Technology has allowed Amazon and Google to succeed where the last generation of conglomerates failed. They organically contain multitudes of media, all deeply integrated within one coherent business. Books, television, newspapers are all a click away from their home pages. Amazon doesn't just make television shows and publish books; it's the vendor that every other media company must use to reach a wide audience; it manufactures devices that no viable publisher and few movie studios can afford to avoid. The company wants us to have the full range of media experiences—sight, sound, and word—in one place, its own.

Old gatekeepers might not always have been worthy of praise, but at least there were a lot of them. And in that multiplicity there was the basis for democracy. In Amazon's vision of the future, there's just one gate. And while Jeff Bezos may wave everyone through, the health of the book business has already come to depend on the whims of one company. Even if he were a benevolent monopolist, that would be a terrifying prospect.

Six

BIG TECH'S
SMOKE-FILLED ROOM

THE ALGORITHM IS A NOVEL PROBLEM for democracy. Technology companies boast, with little shyness, about how they can nudge users toward more virtuous behavior—how they can induce us to click, to read, to buy, or even to vote. These tactics are potent, because we don't see the hand steering us. We don't know how information has been patterned to prod us. Despite all Silicon Valley's sloganeering about building a more transparent world, their ideals stop at the threshold of their offices.

In any other line of business, this secrecy wouldn't much matter. But the knowledge monopolists have unique power in our democracy. They don't just have the ability to pick the fate of a book, they can influence the fate of the Republic. By sorting information, they make decisions that shape our opinions of issues and politicians. Even free-market conservatives will worry about concentrations of power among companies that control the flow of words and ideas, because that power has been so blatantly abused in the past—both the distant past and the not-so-distant past.

Before there was the Internet, there was the telegraph, or what one book dubbed the "Victorian Internet." It's now hard to conjure its long reign. Unlike the radio or the mail, other supposedly antiquated forms of communication, the telegraph was declared lifeless and buried in the graveyard of technology. There was nothing about telegraphy—no charm, no necessity—that could survive change or even persist as a decorative reminder of bygone days. The last telegram was sent in 2006 without elegy.

This little-noted death should not obscure a brilliant life. The telegraph was the first instance of electronic communication. It relayed information instantaneously, across nations and then oceans. When it appeared, the speed and range of the telegraph sparked paroxysms of euphoria, much like the rhapsodic predictions that greeted the arrival of the World Wide Web. Pundits of the mid-nineteenth century credited the newfangled technology with collapsing time and space, rendering distant swaths of geography into a cozy neighborhood. Samuel Morse's famous message, sent from Washington to Baltimore in 1844, trembled in the face of his invention's import: *What Hath God Wrought?*

It took decades—and a catastrophic war—for an answer to Morse's question. When Abraham Lincoln became president, he had seen his first telegraph key only three years earlier. But, in time, he became something of an addict. Sitting in the basement of the War Department, he would send instructions to his generals on the front, a highly personal and highly effective method of command. Over the course of the long war, the Union army strung fifteen thousand miles of telegraph wire, as opposed to the one thousand miles that the rebels managed. This proved an enormous tactical advantage. It allowed for savvy shifting of troops and supplies across the map. When the country exited the war, the telegraph system was national in scale—a tangle of trunks and branches that could quickly relay commercial prices and news. One company, Western Union, was best positioned to privatize this network, and it would come to dominate telegraphy for the next hundred years.

The Western Union monopoly had many accomplices. It received a boost from the government, even before the war. The Congress had created a strong incentive for connecting the two coasts by wire. It granted free use of federal lands for that purpose—and rewarded Western Union with a four-hundred-thousand-dollar bonus when it completed the task in 1861. Western Union wasn't more technologically adept than its competitors; it simply seized the opportunities as they came. When the industry became overcrowded with ill-fated competitors, Western Union swallowed the weaker firms and combined into an implacable behemoth.

At that early moment in the history of the American regulatory state, there were no antitrust laws to constrain Western Union. Still, the company continually dodged political spears. In 1870, the Brits nationalized their telegraph system, housing it within their postal service. Ulysses S. Grant and a raft of politicians openly contemplated doing the same here. Between 1866 and 1900, congressmen introduced seventy bills to have the postal service take over telegraphy.

The success of Western Union, therefore, hinged on its ability to control the terms of the political debate. And its tactics for swaying members of Congress could be quite raw. Until the 1910s, telegraphy was so expensive that only businesses could afford the service. But Western Union wired offices in the Capitol Building and gave elected officials unlimited free use of the system. According to memos in the Western Union archive, the company privately considered this the "cheapest means" of calming its critics in Washington.

Freebies were merely a first line of defense—and relatively innocuous compared with Western Union's other ploys. Its protective shell was the press. More specifically, Western Union formed an impregnable alliance with the Associated Press (AP)— an organization that had achieved an impressive monopoly of its own. The AP supplied American newspapers with an endless stream of copy that helped them to economically fill their pages. Most American newspapers couldn't afford to send correspondents to Washington or Europe, and the AP's network of reporters allowed them to fill that gap. More than 80 percent of the copy in western papers, according to one survey, came from the wire service. Newspapers relied on the AP, and the AP exploited that reliance. It insisted that its clients use no other wire service. Even worse, it insisted that its clients never say a bad public word about the organization.

It was an enviable business model. Certainly, Western Union salivated over the prospect of acquiring a piece of that action. But the optics of the monopolist acquiring even greater power were terrible. So Western Union stumbled upon an even more elegant solution. The two monopolists of the wires would conspire so that they mutually protected each other. Western Union would grant the AP exclusive use of its wires, at a nicely discounted rate. In return, the AP signed a contract that declared that its members would "not in any way encourage or support any opposition or competing telegraph companies." The quid pro quo couldn't have been any clearer. Newspapers that spoke ill of Western Union were tossed from the AP—as was the case with the *Omaha Republican*, punished for having the temerity to describe the telegraph company as an "onerous" and "grievous" monopoly. The alliance of monopolists served its purpose. In his magisterial history of media, Paul Starr has argued, "Unlike the British telegraph companies, Western Union had the press on its side and, in no small measure because of that means of attenuating hostile public opinion, was able to avoid the fate of its British counterparts."

A sense of public duty didn't loom large in the AP's calculus in those years. The AP archives are filled with instances of Republican malfeasance that the organization had uncovered through tips and various other reportorial channels. But the men who ran the AP were rock-ribbed Republicans themselves. The AP chiefs, without a pang of self-consciousness or guilt, committed to burying any evidence of wrongdoing by the leaders of their party.

There's no doubt that many political pundits and reporters have dreamed of making a candidate—taking a ball of political clay and using their journalistic powers to mold a winner. But only the AP had the power to pull off such a mythological assignment. In the election of 1876, the chief of the western branch of the AP, a small, cadaverous man called William Henry Smith, set out to install his friend from Ohio, Governor Rutherford B. Hayes, in the White House. Hayes was no lock for the Republican nomination, let alone greater things. One journalist called him a "third rate nonentity." Still, there was some raw material to work with, as well as brute journalistic force to be deployed. Smith used the AP to paint a glorious image of his candidate. He asked prominent Republican politicians to write glowing private testimonials about Hayes's first-rate character. These missives somehow materialized on the wires and then in papers across the country. Whenever a potentially explosive charge against Hayes surfaced, the AP used overwhelming resources to refute it. (Smith was shrewd, and carefully leaked rumors against Hayes's opponents to newspapers that had no clear connection to him.) So obvious was the propaganda that the organization came to be known as the "Hayesociated Press."

The Hayes campaign was one of American political history's great slogs. It took seven ballots to make him the Republican nominee. And that foreshadowed greater difficulties to come. On election night, Hayes trailed his Democratic opponent, Samuel Tilden, by 250,000 votes. The candidate himself was close to conceding defeat, but he didn't. A *New York Times* editor passed along intelligence that the paper had gleaned from Democratic operatives in the South. In private, the Tilden camp breathed a heavy sigh of relief that Hayes hadn't looked more carefully at the electoral results in three southern states. The vote tally might even have gone Hayes's way and tipped the Electoral College. This intelligence was enough to forestall Hayes's concession. For four months, the result of the election remained hotly contested—so hotly that there were fears that the controversy would culminate in violence and a second civil war. During that long stretch of squabbling, Western Union gave Smith unfettered access to telegrams sent by Democratic strategists. Smith then passed along the purloined information to Hayes—which allowed the Republicans to outmaneuver Tilden and his allies.

Behind the scenes, Associated Press executives helped steer

the negotiations between prudent men of goodwill, on both sides, toward an equitable outcome—that's how they described their grand bargain. In retrospect, the resulting deal was diabolical. Hayes prevailed only when his party agreed to withdraw federal troops from the South. In effect, the Hayes camp had relinquished the dream of reconstructing the South in a spirit of racial equality—the bum deal a small price for installing the AP's man in the White House.

It seems paranoid to fear the repetition of such machinations— and it was certainly easier to pull off a stunt like that more than one hundred years ago, in an era when smoke-filled rooms were the preferred venue for practicing politics. Still, there are lessons that extend to our own time. The owners of powerful companies will always have their own interests and agendas. If they have the means to promote and protect their self-interest and deep beliefs, refraining from the opportunity will require restraint that isn't universally present in human beings. That temptation grows even stronger when technology permits hidden-handed interventions in the political process. It's foolish to believe that it can't happen here, when it already has.

MY OWN SMALL BRUSH with monopoly came at an ill-timed juncture in my career as editor of the *New Republic*. In one hundred years, the magazine had never had a chief executive officer. We had owners who ran the institution with a sense of public mission and personal vanity. (The one year we turned a profit, we celebrated with a pizza party that pushed us back into the red.) But Chris Hughes, the owner of the magazine and my boss, wanted to turn a profit. He freely admitted that it required greater business acumen than he possessed, or than he could hire without offering a big, enticing title.

The thing about CEOs is that they have "chief" in their title, and with that the implied power to fire the editor. I found that an unsettling shift in the chain of command. (Before the arrival of the CEO, I had reported directly to Chris.) It seemed somewhat unpromising that the new CEO waited nearly two weeks to meet with me after starting. There were, however, mitigating circumstances. I worked in Washington, the magazine's main editorial office, and he worked in New York, where we housed our business side. I clung to that fact and held out hope that I might persist into the new regime.

After my first meeting with the CEO, I wasn't so sure. His name was Guy Vidra, an alumnus of various tech start-ups, with the requisite Fitbit around his wrist, rectangular spectacles, and trimmed facial hair. He came to us, most recently, by way of Yahoo! As I entered his office, this suddenly seemed like an entirely different planet.

I was hoping for a bit of get-to-know-you chat as I sank down into a low-slung leather chair in his office and then leaned forward into a posture of hyper-agreeability. My mission was to charm him and persuade him of my commercial spirit. But before I could begin to court him, he rose from behind his walnut-and-steel desk, grabbed a marker, and headed to the whiteboard on his wall. "Here's what I'm thinking," he said as he began to sketch a plan for remaking the editorial structure of the magazine. I saw an incomprehensible tangle of arrows and circles quickly materialize. But as he spoke, I caught the drift. What attracted Vidra was the transformation of the *New Republic* into a technology company with the ethos of a start-up. This required an overhaul of our mission and core character.

My reputation in the office was as a nostalgist and traditionalist. I liked to tell the story of how my father had turned me into a reader of the *New Republic* by slipping his finished issues under my bedroom door. And I had just edited a centennial anthology of writings from the magazine's back catalog. This reputation reinforced an impression that I resented: Vidra considered me insensitive to the imperative to make money. I certainly didn't mean to confirm this impression. But the magazine had a void in its cover lineup, and I quickly pulled together an essay on Amazon.

This was the fall of 2014—and contract negotiations between Amazon and the publishing giant Hachette had grown protracted and foul. I hadn't much cared about the early months of the contretemps, which pitted a monopoly against an oligopoly. Neither side struck me as worthy of huge sympathy. But then the battle-front encroached uncomfortably close to home. I watched as Amazon punished Hachette's writers in its effort to make the publisher feel pain. Books, the products of years of passionate labor, were prevented from reaching the market. Amazon used its bully's arm to delay their shipments or direct readers to older books on similar subjects, as well as a raft of other vengeful tactics. It's a failure of moral imagination that writers respond only to injustices that they can envision suffering themselves. But I had published with Hachette and it wasn't hard to make the empathetic leap that landed me in solidarity with the writers whose sales Amazon crashed.

My essay appeared under a headline that had fists. The cover blared, "Amazon Must Be Stopped." The piece described why the government should get tough with Amazon for transgressing antitrust laws. It found an audience, but fairly quickly receded from the forefront of my mind. Attention was pretty clearly needed elsewhere. My intraoffice campaign for survival seemed to be floundering. One afternoon, I sat at my computer as I received email from six different media reporters seeking to confirm rumors that I was about to be fired. "This isn't the most comfortable question, but here goes . . ."

It was at that awkward moment that Amazon decided that it would punish the *New Republic*. Our ad sales department received a note, informing us that Amazon would be yanking its advertising for its new political comedy, *Alpha House*. The missive left nothing to the imagination. "In light of the cover article about Amazon, Amazon has decided to terminate the *Alpha House* campaign currently running on the *New Republic*. Please confirm receipt of this email and that the campaign has been terminated." It was signed, "Team Amazon."

When I asked Chris Hughes if I could pick a fight over Amazon's cancellation, he sent me a curt note instructing me to remain quiet. Unfortunately, I had already forwarded Amazon's note to a friend—who, in turn, excitedly and unadvisedly forwarded it to the *New York Times*. Before I could stuff the controversy back into a quiet corner, a reporter had written Chris asking him to comment. While my boss was fuming at my disobedience, I was sitting on a cross-country flight from San Francisco with painfully slow WiFi. I sent an email furiously pleading with my friend to help make the story go away. I could hear the backswing of the executioner.

We shouldn't be hyperbolic about the knowledge monopolies.

The Associated Press's schemes from the nineteenth century are an extreme case. Most media barons don't aspire to rig presidential elections. Their interests are far more parochial. In this way, they are no different from any other big business. They want to stave off the regulators and the tax man; they want to protect their business from the incursions of government, and to inhale government largesse, when profit can be made.

But, then again, knowledge monopolists are not like every other business. Every writer, every media outlet, every book publisher depends on these companies for their financial survival. These companies, therefore, have a unique ability to inhibit criticism of themselves. They don't need to lift a finger to ward off naysayers. By virtue of their size, the fact that they dominate much of the market for disseminating ideas, criticizing them often seems like a suicidal gesture.

After writing my essay on Amazon, I crossed from critic to activist. I accompanied the Authors Guild on trips to the Federal Trade Commission and the Justice Department to discuss the perils of Amazon's size. These meetings were private. That condition provided the safety that permitted writers to make the trip to Washington to press their case against Amazon. I assumed that any writer willing to blare complaints at the U.S. government would be willing to blare those complaints in public.

This was the one way in which I had significantly underestimated the power of Jeff Bezos. When I worked with colleagues to put together a conference on Amazon at a center-left think tank, some of our comrades suddenly lost their nerve. They had books on the way. There was no way that they would risk their hard work by attaching their name to the cause. Loss of nerve was hardly an isolated incident. When we asked a Washington lawyer to speak at the event, it didn't matter that he had a long record of crossing swords with big companies. "I think I'm going to pass for personal reasons," he wrote. "My daughter has been working on a book that her agent will send out to publishers shortly. So, the manuscript will be under consideration at about the same time as your program. The publishers are so paranoid about what Amazon could do that I think it might affect their behavior. So, I think that I need to keep a lower profile on this one at this stage." This logic flabbergasted me. I called a literary agent to relay the incident. The agent had delivered anti-Amazon zingers to reporters over the years, but he surprised me with his fatalism. "You've done your bit," he told me, just before hanging up. "It's important to consider your own interests now."

Amazon is hardly immune from public outcry. The *New York Times* has rigorously reported on the company. And there's safety in numbers. When activist groups circulate letters criticizing Amazon, plenty of writers sign them. Still, it's possible to catch a glimpse of a more frigid future that follows the current arc toward monopoly. Even if Amazon behaves in saintly fashion, its size will intimidate. Courage doesn't grow if one glances over at the *Washington Post*. Since Bezos bought it, the paper has hardly replicated the *Times'* tough coverage. Bezos could have declared that he deserves the same treatment that the paper dishes out to the rest of the world. Instead, the paper tiptoes around him, which seems to be the way he likes it.

This might seem like a minor point. But as Amazon continues its march, its ambition keeps expanding. It wants to populate the skies with drones. It will provide the essential technological infrastructure for governments. It will set the tone for the future of the workplace and the future of the economy, as well as the future of the culture. Amazon's power isn't an incidental subject for public debate; it is an essential one.

THE HARVARD LAW PROFESSOR Jonathan Zittrain has spun the following hypothetical scenario. There's a down-to-the-wire election. Mark Zuckerberg has a strong opinion about the candidate he would like to prevail. As we have seen, Facebook claims that it can boost voter turnout, carefully placing reminders of civic duty in News Feeds on Election Day, generating social pressure to head to the polls. That this experiment worked isn't just a public relations claim, but an established finding of social science. In the Zittrain scenario, Zuckerberg launches another get-out-the-vote effort. Only this time, the reminders are placed selectively. Facebook has a pretty good sense of your political affiliation, based on all the items you've liked. Facebook can also discern your voting precinct. So instead of urging all citizens to perform their civic duty, Facebook calibrates its call to action to target only the voters who will pull the lever for Zuckerberg's candidate.

The idea that a tech company would favor a candidate is hardly novel. Google's executive chairman, Eric Schmidt, threw himself behind Barack Obama in the 2012 election. He muddied himself in the arcane details of the campaign, not just writing checks, but recruiting talent and helping build its technological apparatus. His recruits scoured massive data sets to target voters with unprecedented precision. "On election night he was in our boiler room," says Obama campaign guru David Plouffe. These efforts made a difference. "Obama campaign veterans say that applying this rigor to their half-billion-dollar media budget made it 15 percent more efficient, saving tens of millions of dollars," *Bloomberg* reported after the campaign.

This wasn't just a freelance effort. Google published a case study about the role it played in re-electing the president, titled "Obama for America uses Google Analytics to democratize rapid, data-driven decision making." The paper has attracted barely any attention, but contains brash claims about Google's centrality to the outcome of the election. "Early on, [the Obama campaign] turned to Google Analytics to help the web, email, and ads teams understand what motivated new supporters to become more vocal advocates and regular donors over time." Google boasted about how its data helped the Obama campaign shape the information voters turned up when they wanted to verify claims made during debates, and as they mulled their choices in the days leading up to the election. "Real-Time reports in Google Analytics provided the campaign a window into voters' questions and concerns, and allowed them to deliver answers directly from the campaign through search ads." Google was hardly modest in assessing how it contributed to the campaign's success: "The results from Election Day speak for themselves: a resounding victory, with nearly every battleground state falling into the President's column."

We don't need to assume the worst about the tech companies to fear their capacity to swing votes. As we have seen from the Edward Snowden saga, a rogue programmer can find ways to undermine highly secure systems. Marius Milner, an engineer at Google, abused his access to Google's street-mapping vehicles. These cars traversed the roadways of America, taking pictures, which Google would stitch together into a coherent view. Milner programmed Google's cars to tap the WiFi signals coming from the homes they passed, sweeping up private data, even email correspondence. Instead of cooperating with a government investigation, Google "deliberately impeded and delayed," earning a fine from the Federal Communications Commission in the process. Indeed, the company refrained from firing Milner. The case hardly builds confidence in Google's commitment to transparency or in its safeguards against abuse.

It wouldn't take much for a search engine to tip public opinion. One study, published in the *Proceedings of the National Academy of Sciences*, attempted to simulate the workings of Google. Researchers rigged up a fake search engine, which they called Kadoodle, and simulated a phony election with phony candidates. In the experiment, the authors kept reordering search results and then asking respondents to divulge their opinion. Placement in the search engine, it turns out, matters a lot: "On all measures, opinions shifted in the direction of the candidate who was favored in the rankings. Trust, liking and voting preferences all shifted predictably."

WE USED TO BE highly intolerant of media's subterranean attempts to shape us, even in commercial contexts. In 1973, ads for a board game called Hūsker Dū? attempted to goose Christmas sales. The words "get it" flashed so quickly across the TV screen that nobody would ever have noticed. But when the owners of the ad agency that cut the spots learned that their minions had slipped in the subliminal message without any authorization, they panicked and informed the networks of its presence. Word of the stunt leaked and a national furor ensued. There's no evidence that subliminal messaging of this sort actually works. Nevertheless, the government decided that it wouldn't abide subliminal messaging. It amounted to a form of deception and a violation of the public's trust. Soon after the Hüsker Dü? kerfuffle, the FCC declared the practice "contrary to the public interest." With the rise of the big technology companies, we've turned away from that view. We've accepted a whole new level of subconscious manipulation of our behavior. But where televised subliminal messaging was ultimately meaningless, the new behaviorism is highly effective, and therefore plausibly dangerous.

Transparency is one of the great promises of new technology, and with transparency we're meant to enter a new age of accountability. Yet the knowledge monopolies take us in the other direction. They contain the trappings of openness—customers who can shout back at companies, the space to blare an unpopular opinion, a world seemingly without human gatekeepers. But if you stare hard enough at Google, Facebook, and Amazon they become a bit like Italy, a country where it's never entirely clear how power really operates. Rules exist but are never convincingly spelled out. We have a dim awareness that we're being subconsciously influenced, but never know when and how. We see some types of information given more favorable treatment, but not for any explicit reason. Though the tech companies preach liberal values, they crave access to markets in authoritarian countries, where compromise with ugly regimes is the cost of doing business. Facebook has shown how noble sentiment doesn't preclude collaboration with the censor. Would they ever do the same here? The threat to our democracy may never be more than a theoretical one. Then again, how will we ever know?

The failure to internalize—or perhaps even comprehend— the meaning of their own rhetoric about transparency is characteristic. American democracy was built on richly deserved fear, an anxiety that power might pool in one institution at everyone else's expense. The tech companies have no such fear. The more they can insinuate themselves into our lives the better. There is no limit. Of course, it's not their job to worry about their power. That anxiety falls to the rest of us, and we should be far clearer about the problem: Companies that are indifferent to democracy have acquired an outsized role in it.

WORLD WITHOUT MIND

Seven

THE VIRALITY VIRUS

JOURNALISTS HAVE AN ANNOYING TENDENCY to insert themselves in the center of the narrative. They assume that their problems are the world's problems, that their conversations with a taxi driver reflect the totality of human experience. This narcissism makes it hard to see the moments when journalism's plight is actually emblematic of American economic life.

Over the last generation, journalism has slowly been swallowed. The ascendant media companies of our era don't think of themselves as heirs to a great ink-stained tradition. Some prefer to call themselves technology firms. This redefinition isn't just a bit of fashionable branding. Silicon Valley has infiltrated the profession, from both within and without. Over the past decade, journalism has come to depend unhealthily on Facebook and Google. The big tech companies supply journalism with an enormous percentage of its audience—and therefore a big chunk of revenue. This gives Silicon Valley influence over the entire profession, and it has made the most of its power.

Dependence generates desperation—a mad, shameless chase to gain clicks through Facebook, a relentless effort to game Google's algorithms. It leads media to ink terrible deals, which look like self-preserving necessities, but really just allow Facebook and Google to hold them even tighter. Media will grant Facebook the right to sell advertising or give Google permission to publish articles directly on its fast-loading server. What makes these deals so terrible is the capriciousness of the tech companies. They like to shift quickly in a radically different direction, which is great for their bottom line, but terrible for all the media companies dependent on the platforms. Facebook will decide that its users prefer video to words, or that its users prefer ideologically pleasing propaganda to hard news. When Facebook shifts direction like this or when Google tweaks its algorithm, they instantly crash Web traffic flowing to media, with all the rippling revenue ramifications that follow. Media know they should flee the grasp of Facebook, but dependence also breeds cowardice. The prisoner lies on the cot dreaming of escape plans that will never hatch.

Dependence on the big tech companies is increasingly the plight of the worker and the entrepreneur. Drivers maintain erratic patterns of sleep because of Uber's shifting whims. Companies that manufacture tchotchkes sold on Amazon watch their businesses collapse when Amazon's algorithms detect the profitability of their item, leading the giant to manufacture the goods itself at a lower price. The problem isn't just financial vulnerability. It's the way in which the tech companies dictate the patterns of work, the way in which their influence can shift the ethos of an entire profession to suit their needs—lowering standards of quality, eroding ethical protections. I saw this up close during my time at the *New Republic*. I watched how dependence on the tech companies undermined the very integrity of journalism. At the very beginning of that chapter in my career, I never imagined that we would go down that path.

CHRIS HUGHES WAS A MYTHICAL SAVIOR—boyishly innocent, fantastically rich, intellectually curious, unexpectedly humble, and proudly idealistic. My entire career at the *New Republic* had been spent dreaming of such a benefactor. For many years, we drifted from one ownership group to the next, each eager to save the magazine and its historic mission. But these investors either lacked the resources to invest in our future or didn't have quite enough faith to fully commit. We kept cranking out magazines, but haunted by the specter of getting offloaded to a Russian oligarch or an ideological fanatic. It was an unending search for patronage that exhausted me. I resigned as editor in 2010. A year later, the *New Republic* entered yet another pressing hunt for a new owner. And then Chris walked through the door.

When Chris first invited me for a chat, we wandered aimlessly across downtown Washington, paper coffee cups in our hands. It was a jacketless day in earliest spring. We settled on the stone steps of a Georgian church. In those first weeks of his ownership, Chris booked himself an endless listening tour. He seemed eager to speak with anyone who had worked at the magazine, or might have a strong opinion about it. But as we talked, it seemed clear that he wanted something more than my advice. He began to hint that he might want me to return to my old job.

The owners of the *New Republic* had always been older men,

who had settled into their wealth and strong opinions. Chris was intriguingly different. He was twenty-eight years old, and his enthusiasm for learning made him feel even younger. "When I first heard the *New Republic* was for sale," he told me, "I went to the New York Public Library and began to read." He ordered up microfiche from the stacks. From each decade of the magazine's hundred-year existence, he selected a year's worth of issues to plow through. The romance of the magazine's history—its storied slate of writers, Rebecca West, Virginia Woolf, Edmund Wilson, Ralph Ellison, James Wood—ignited his imagination and loosened his hold on his wallet.

College had been a blur, he explained. His Harvard roommate Mark Zuckerberg had hatched Facebook. This proximity proved lucrative beyond any plausible dream. Chris became the company's first head of publicity, even though he remained in Cambridge as his buddies decamped to Silicon Valley. But that was Chris. He always spoke of Facebook with an endearing detachment. "I don't spend much time on the site," he once confessed over dinner. Besides, the source of his fortune didn't define him. What he really loved was literature. During his honeymoon, he read *War and Peace*; he would sit waiting for appointments with an edition of Balzac in the original French. The leather ottoman in his SoHo apartment was topped with piles of the *New York Review of Books*, and seemingly every literary journal published in the English language. The *New Republic* was going to be the liberal arts experience he was too distracted to enjoy at Harvard.

Despite having hundreds of millions in stock, he seemed indifferent to his wealth, or at least conflicted by it. He would get red-faced when people pointed out that he owned two estates and a spacious loft; he was apt to wear the same blazer every day of the week. So much positive media attention had flowed in his direction, he saw no need to cultivate more. At meetings, he would quietly recede. He hated the idea of fixing himself at the head of the table and pontificating, which had been a long-standing perk of owning the *New Republic*.

As we sat on the steps, he began to lay out his plans for the magazine. It felt a bit restrained and a little aimless, a mélange of incremental improvements, adding an interview, shortening book reviews.

"Why aren't you being bolder?" I asked.

"Show me how to be bolder," he replied.

MANY MONTHS LATER, our relationship would sour, but our first days working together were exhilarating. As a brash outsider, he had no interest in blindly adhering to received wisdom. When we set out to rebuild the *New Republic*'s Web site, we talked ourselves into striking a reactionary stance. Instead of chasing traffic, our home page would aggressively eschew such notions. We would resist the impulse to clutter it with an endless stream of clicky content, splayed with little sense of hierarchy. Our digital pages would prize beauty and finitude; they would sacrifice any ambitions for a broad audience and would brashly announce the idealism of our project—which he would describe as nothing less than the preservation of cultural seriousness and long-form journalism.

Romantic idealism wasn't enough to satisfy Chris. He always believed that he could turn the *New Republic* into a profitable enterprise—or at least grow revenue enough that he could trumpet his success in press releases that would make us an even hotter book. But Chris's rhetoric about profit never seemed entirely sincere. "I hate selling ads," he would tell me over and over. "It makes me feels seedy." And for more than a year, he was willing to spend with abandon.

With the benefit of hindsight, I should have been more disciplined about the checks we, I mean *he*, wrote. It wasn't hard to foresee the inevitable frustration that would emerge when he finally paid close attention to the financials. But he had a weakness for leasing offices in prime locations and hiring top-shelf consultants. I had a weakness for handsomely paying writers to travel the globe, commissioning pieces as if I were a fancy New York editor. Since the window of his beneficence would surely close, I moved quickly to hire a large staff, which included experienced writers and editors who didn't come cheap. But he didn't seem to mind. "I've never been so happy or fulfilled," Chris would tell me. "I'm working with friends."

Then one day it happened. The numbers caught up with Chris, and he felt an urgent and understandable need to make revenue appear. Since Chris didn't care for advertising, he refused to pay top dollar for a sales force that would hawk the magazine to the agencies. Money needed to come from somewhere—and that somewhere was the Web. A dramatic increase in traffic would bring the revenue that would close the gap. (We would be relying on programmatic advertising, the algorithmically driven auctions that advertisers use to buy access to desirable demographics cheaply, regardless of the sites where their ads run.) We were suddenly living a microcosm of recent media history in a time-elapsed sequence that collapsed a decade of painful transition into a few tense months. Our digital revolution couldn't happen quickly enough.

When Chris hired me, he was under no illusions. Despite starting at *Slate*, I wasn't what they call a "digital native." The Web interested me; the hunt for traffic piqued my competitive tendencies. None of this, however, was my passion. Chris, on the other hand, was a founding father of social media. Although he didn't care to be defined by that fact, he was a fixture at panels on digital media. He not only felt urgency about the necessity of traffic, but knew the tricks to make it happen.

Growing traffic required a new mind-set. Unlike television, the ethos of print journalism shunned the strategic pursuit of audience as a dirty, somewhat corrupting enterprise. Or that pursuit was something best left to the business side, not a concern for writers and editors. The *New Republic* held an extreme version of this belief. It had been born as an elite magazine—an invention of Progressive Era intellectuals who hoped to elevate the cultural and political standards of the country. Over the decades, it became something close to a cult, catering to the small group that wanted to read insider writing about politics and highbrow meditations on books. This admixture never made for the most robust audience. For most of its long history, the readership of the *New Republic* couldn't fill the University of Mississippi's football stadium. Suddenly, we needed to develop our Web site to reach millions of readers; we needed to ditch our elitism and meet the masses where they lived.

A LARGER AUDIENCE WAS CLEARLY within reach. That was the lesson that journalism was absorbing. We could even reduce the lesson to a mathematical equation. Jonah Peretti, the founder of Buzz-Feed and the William Randolph Hearst of our era, has expressed it this way: R = ζ.* The formula supposedly illustrates how a piece of editorial content could go viral—how it could travel through the social networks to quickly reach a massive audience, as rapidly as smallpox ripped its way across North America. Peretti's formula, in fact, came from epidemiology. The nod to science was intentional. With experimentation and careful reading of data, science could suggest which pieces had the best shot at achieving virality—and if not virality, then at least a robust audience.

The emerging science of traffic was really a branch of behavioral psychology—people clicked so quickly, they didn't always fully understand why they gravitated to one piece over another. They were moved by cognitive biases, irrational forces, decisions made in a semiconscious state. So enticing a reader might entail a little manipulation, a little hidden persuasion.

Chris had learned the science of virality from a site called Upworthy. He had supplied money to help launch Upworthy and turn it into an Internet sensation—"the fastest-growing media start-up in memory," as one of many fawning press stories described it. Upworthy didn't produce much of anything original. It plucked videos and graphics from across the Web, usually obscure stuff, then gave them headlines that made them appealing to the widest audience. This content was meant to have a progressive sensibility—at the intersection of "awesome" and "meaningful." Upworthy took the raw material of others and gave it the magical elements that yielded virality.

Magical isn't the right word. Psychologists had discovered

---

* In epidemiology, the ζ represents the number of people who come in contact with a contagious individual, while β represents the probability of transmission.

that a state of unquenchable curiosity could be cultivated. Humans are comfortable with ignorance, but they hate feeling deprived of information. Upworthy designed headlines to make readers feel an almost primal hunger for information just outside their grasp. It pioneered a style—which it called the "curiosity gap"—that explicitly teased readers, withholding just enough information to titillate the reader into going further. Classic example: "9 out of 10 Americans Are Completely Wrong About This Mind-Blowing Fact." Six million readers couldn't contain themselves and followed that link. (The mind-blowing fact: income inequality is far worse than most Americans think.)

The headline is, of course, an ancient journalistic art form. But Upworthy—and its legions of imitators—subjected it to positivistic rigor. With every item it posted, Upworthy would write twenty-five different headlines. Software allowed Upworthy to automatically publish all twenty-five, and then determine the most clickable of the bunch. Based on these results, Upworthy uncovered syntactical patterns that were close to sure hits. (Upworthy found tremendous success when it used variations of the sentence "You Won't Believe What Happened Next.") These formulas were so effective that they became commonplace across the Web—so overused that readers grew wise to the tricks and the formulas lost their powers, which led to the frantic scramble to discover the next new thing.

The core insight of Upworthy, BuzzFeed, Vox, and the other emerging Internet behemoths was that editorial success could be engineered—that if you listened to the data, it was possible to craft pieces that would win massive audiences. This was an insight embraced across the industry, even at sober places like the *Washington Post*. And it was an insight the wormed its way into the *New Republic*. Chris installed a data guru on our staff to in-crease our odds of producing viral hits. In weekly meetings, the guru would come armed with topics that we would be wise to pursue. He would keep a careful eye on the topics trending on Facebook, so that we could create content that might ride a wave of popularity. He looked back on historical data to see what the public craved a year ago, so that we could produce pieces in sync with the seasonal interests of readers. "Super Bowl ads are big," he told us. "What can we create to hit that moment?" Or "Chipotle has run out of pork and it's all over social. What can we gener-ate?" Questions like these were usually greeted by hostile silence.

While I didn't care for the tactics, I didn't strenuously resist them either. Chris still encouraged us to publish long essays and deeply reported pieces. A few schlocky baubles seemed a small price to pay. What's more, he asked a perfectly reasonable ques-tion. Respectable media were going down this path. Did we really think we were better than *Time* or the *Washington Post*? They had all adopted a genre that he called "snackable content"—these were charts, lists, videos, quick items that would appeal to the "bored at work crowd," as the industry termed it, or to the folks killing time on the subway platform. To be sure, the subject could be serious, but the presentation had to be fast and fun, geared to spread via Facebook. Chris was adamant about the necessity of producing this kind of work, because the methods for producing snackable content were so obvious—and, in his view, required little effort. We simply had to mimic the rest of the Internet—write about the same outrage as everyone else, jump on the same topic of the moment. Clicks would rain down upon us if only we could get over ourselves and post the same short clips from *The Daily Show* as everyone else, framed by an appealing headline and perhaps a conscience-salving paragraph or two of analysis. A Jon Stewart rant was can't-miss stuff. It was hard to argue with his logic. Everyone else was doing this. They were doing it because it worked. We needed things to work.

THE *NEW REPUBLIC* COULDN'T RESIST the historical force remaking our profession, and neither could most other outlets. Silicon Valley has succeeded in bending journalism to its whims, because journalism is weak. Or let's put it more charitably: Journalism likes to pose as a pillar of the Republic, which it may be, but it's a newly planted pillar and not so firmly embedded in the soil. American newspapers have existed for 250 years—but the idea that journalists would write the news without partisan bias, in a professional manner, is a newfangled thing, hardly a century old.

Until recently, the narrative of American journalism could be told as a story of triumphant progress. It began in a swamp of partisan bombast, where even stiff-collared papers like the *New York Times* and the *Washington Post* were full of invective. (The *Post* started as a mouthpiece of the Democratic Party, created to hound Rutherford B. Hayes—whom it referred to as "His Fraudulency.") But partisanship was just a toddler phase for the press. Before newspapers could enter into respectability, they needed to go through an adolescence of sensationalism. Over the course of the nineteenth century, a new generation of press barons (William Randolph Hearst, Joseph Pulitzer) came to see the massive profits to be made in yellow journalism—overhyped, tawdry stories about crime and gossip, with lavish illustrations and blunt headlines. The sensationalist press generated sizable audiences— a large mass of consumers who could be persuaded to buy the new products rolling out of the factories and sold in urban department stores. "The pull of dollars towards sensationalism helped move newspapers away from the political parties," the media historian Michael Schudson writes.

Commercialism had a strange, unexpected consequence. Only after newspapers came to depend on the market for survival did journalism self-consciously reject the pressures of the market. Journalism came to insist on its objectivity, to describe its mission as nothing less than the pursuit of Truth. There were sociological reasons for this new high-mindedness. Advertising created an explosion of newspapers—and that swelled the ranks of writers and editors. The employees of newspapers aspired to join the ranks of the respectable professions. Instead of shading the truth and spouting opinions, newspaper writers began to view themselves as "reporters"—faithfully recounting reality. Interviewing was an esoteric practice in the mid-nineteenth century; by World War I, it was an essential part of the job. Advertisers liked the idea of professionalism, too. They preferred to sell their wares next to the least controversial, least alienating copy possible. And though owners might rather have used papers as their own playthings, they came to accept the new way of neutral just-the-facts reporting—which gave their papers (and themselves) a new legitimacy.

The essential text of the era was Walter Lippmann's *Liberty and the News*, which he published in 1920. As an ambitious young editor at the *New Republic*, Lippmann had supported the Great War, but the public's response to the conflict horrified him. He never expected the surge of raw, ugly xenophobia that followed Wilson's call to arms. It was a "reign of terror" fed by a "hurricane of demagogy." The sheer ignorance of the public horrified him, and he pinned blame on the press. "In an exact sense the present crisis of western democracy is a crisis in journalism." Modern life had grown dizzying. Propaganda and distortion stood in the way of the average citizen's search for truth. Lippmann, an unabashed elitist, saw the reinvention of the press as one of society's most urgent tasks. Journalism may have been headed toward professionalism, but Lippmann demanded that it step up the pace. He called for the creation of journalism schools, for a new standard of rigor, and above all, for a collective commitment to the ideal of objectivity.

By the time newspapers emerged from World War II, they conveyed a sense of permanence, a marble edifice. It was as if they had always acted with such noble purpose. With this sense of self-importance, there was a dismissiveness toward their paid audience—they were considered almost incidental. Robert Darnton, who wrote for the *Times* in the sixties, has recalled, "We really wrote for one another. . . . We knew that no one would jump on our stories as quickly as our colleagues; for reporters make the most voracious readers, and they have to win their status anew each day as they expose themselves before their peers in print." This sense of elitism and purpose helped insulate the American press from pernicious pressures. It made the American newspaper unusually sober. Relative to the rest of the world, the American newspaper proved resistant to corruption and sensationalism. That was a strong belief, but it is now severely tested by pressure emanating from all sides.

At the beginning of the century, the profession was in extremis. A series of recessions prodded media companies to gamble everything on a digital future, a future unencumbered by the clunky, bureaucratic apparatus of publishing on paper. The sense of crisis and opportunity quickly remade the old newsrooms. Over the course of a decade, journalism shed $1.6 billion worth of reporter and editor salaries. At the same time that journalism shriveled, its prestige collapsed. One survey ranked newspaper reporter as the worst job in America, edging out lumberjack and parole officer. It was an existential crisis that caused the profession to reconsider its very reasons for existing. All those nostrums about independence suddenly seemed like an unaffordable luxury. Generating revenue was a goal that reporters could no longer blithely ignore.

This was a dangerous turn. Journalism had never been a public-spirited enterprise, really. That was just a myth that editors and writers liked to tell themselves. Yet the myth mattered. It pushed journalism to challenge power, made it loath to bend to the whims of its audience; it provided a crucial sense of detachment. That myth is in the process of being shredded.

ONE OF THE EMBLEMS of the new era hung over my life at the *New Republic*. It dogged me across my day. Every time I sat down to work, I surreptitiously peeked at it—and I did so as I woke up in the morning, then a few minutes later when I brushed my teeth, and again later in the day as I stood at the urinal. Sometimes I would just stare at the meter's gyrations, neglecting the piece I was editing or ignoring the person seated across my desk. My viewership was often wishful. I hoped that the meter would unexpectedly surge, an illustration of my genius for picking a winner.

My master was called Chartbeat, a site that provides editors, writers, and their bosses with a real-time accounting of Web traffic, showing the flickering readership of each and every article. The site pretty clearly implied that journalism is a competition, a popularity contest. The site's needle made us feel as if our magazine were a car, showing us either sputtering up the hill of a poor traffic day or cruising to a satisfying number.

This is the familiar story of the American workplace. Analytics are the managerial revolution of our time. We live in a world of ubiquitous data that provide the basis for ever greater efficiency and productivity, if only we learn from the numbers. This is the reason that Chartbeat and an array of its competitors have taken such hold in virtually every magazine, newspaper, and blog. The point of Chartbeat is that no piece has sufficient traffic—it can always be improved with a bit of tweaking, a better headline, a better approach to social media, a better subject, a better argument. Like a manager standing over the assembly line with a stopwatch, Chartbeat and its ilk have come to hover over the newsroom. The *Washington Post* (and after I left, the *New Republic*) installed giant television screens that display traffic stats to the staff. Jonah Peretti boasted, "A lot of what we do at BuzzFeed is give dashboards to every person who works at BuzzFeed where they're seeing how people are engaging with the content they're producing: Is it going up? Is it going down?"

This generation of media giants, born on the Internet, has no patience for journalism's old ethos of detachment. It's not that these companies don't have aspirations toward journalistic greatness. BuzzFeed, *Vice*, and the *Huffington Post* want to be postmodern newspapers. They invest in excellent reporting and have first-rate journalists on their staffs. But these companies don't try to insulate themselves from the pressures of the market. Their pursuit of audience—winning the popularity contest of the Web—is central to their mission. They have allowed the endless feedback loop of the Web—the never-ending flood of data—to shape their editorial sensibility, to determine their editorial investments.

Take BuzzFeed, which briefly pushed a strategy that it called "no haters." Negative stories, it concluded, didn't have a fighting shot at virality. Jonah Peretti put it with characteristic clarity: "If something is a total bummer, people don't share it. . . . The problem is, after looking at that you feel depressed. . . . It's almost like you're sending a bad feeling to your friends so why would you want to send a bad feeling to your friends?" The words of Nick Denton, the evil genius behind *Gawker*, which was eventually sued into oblivion, are even more clarifying: "Nobody wants to eat the boring vegetables. Nor does anyone want to pay to encourage people to eat their vegetables. But, anyway, look at me. I used to cover political reform in post-communist Eastern Europe, which had been my subject at Oxford. And now I tell writers that the numbers (i.e. the audience) won't support any worthiness. We can't even write stories about moguls like Rupert Murdoch or Barry Diller unless it involves photographs of them cavorting with young flesh. (I used to enjoy those stories in the old days, before web metrics.)"

It's a vulgar approach, and a triumphant one. We can see its influence in the way that the *New York Times* has openly salivated over BuzzFeed's success. Three years ago, the *Times* ordered an "Innovation Report"—an internal document that inevitably escaped the confines of the building and found its way to the Internet. The report flayed the paper for failing to vigorously compete on the Web. It was an unusually self-flagellating document, especially because the *Times* had built a technologically sophisticated site. Yet there were causes for consternation. The *Times* had entered the Web's popularity contest, but hardly realized that fact.

It hadn't hitched itself to data and analytics with the same fervor as BuzzFeed, which meant that it really had no clue about mastering the Internet. It produced the odd hits for the Web, but never bothered creating templates to replicate them. Above all, the paper clung to the old ethos of journalism, the one that fended off the business side, that fretted about poisoning the pursuit of truth with the pursuit of profit. "The very first step, however, should be a deliberate push to abandon our current metaphors of choice—'The Wall' and 'Church and State'—which project an enduring need for division," the authors of the report declared.

The report was right to describe the *Times'* conservative values, and we should be thankful for that fact. Though the *Times* has taken steps in the direction of BuzzFeed, it has resisted revolutionary change and it remains the most excellent paper in the world. But the point isn't that the descent toward conformity and dreck will happen in a flash. Professional norms, and only professional norms, protect journalism. With sustained hectoring and pressure from above, the norms can be ground to bits. Once they disappear, journalism will be over.

THE ESSENTIAL TERM of this media era is "trending." Facebook and Twitter feature it—a list of the subjects in the process of becoming ubiquitous. And the big media organizations have a sophisticated set of analytic tools—a service called CrowdTangle, for example—that alerts them to trending topics at the trailhead of their ascent to popularity. Once a story grabs attention, media mindlessly glom on to it. They write about the topic with repetitive fury, milking the subject for clicks until the public loses interest.

A memorable yet utterly forgettable example: A boastful photo of a Minnesota hunter smiling above the corpse of a lion called Cecil generated more than 3.2 million stories. Every news organization—even the *New York Times* and the *New Yorker*—attempted to generate hysteria, so that it could scrape some traffic from it. This required finding some novel angle—or a just-novel-enough angle. Vox: "Eating Chicken Is Morally Worse Than Killing Cecil the Lion." BuzzFeed: "A Psychic Says She Spoke with Cecil the Lion." The *Atlantic*: "From Cecil the Lion to Climate Change: A Perfect Storm of Outrage." And so on, a deluge of ephemera dissecting the ephemeral.

In some ways, this is just a digitally enhanced version of an old-fashioned media pile-on: an explosion of moralistic furor, thoroughly exploited. But social media amplify the financial incentive to join the herd. Even the littlest magazine has the possibility of achieving virality, of attracting millions of readers, if it can package its stories shrewdly. Higher-brow publications have no guilt about tossing off articles on these trending subjects, so long as they dress them up a bit with a pocket square of academic pretension or a scarf of argumentative cleverness. The results are highly derivative. As in Hollywood, time and money get poured into a formulaic product, a cautious imitation of past successes. Joshua Topolsky, a founder of Vox Media and The Verge, bemoaned this creeping homogenization: "Everything looks the same, reads the same, and seems to be competing for the same eyeballs."

The problem isn't just the media's dependence on Silicon Valley companies. It's the dependence on Silicon Valley values. Just like the tech companies, journalism has come to fetishize data. And this data has come to corrupt journalism. Reporters and their bosses can assert otherwise. They can pretend to rise above the information, to selectively ignore the numbers and continue the relentless pursuit of higher truths and nobler interests. But data is a Pandora's box. Once journalists come to know what works, which stories yield traffic, they will pursue what works. This is the definition of pandering and it has horrific consequences.

Donald Trump is the culmination of the era. He understood how, more than at any moment in recent history, media need to give the public what it wants, a circus that exploits subconscious tendencies and biases. Even if media disdained Trump's outrages, they built him up as a character and a plausible candidate. For years, media pumped Trump's theories about President Obama's foreign birth into circulation, even though they were built on dunes of crap. It gave endless attention to his initial smears of immigrants, even though media surely understood how those provocations stoked an atmosphere of paranoia and hate. Once Trump became a plausible candidate, media had no choice but to cover him. But media had carried him to that point. Stories about Trump yielded the sort of traffic that pleased the Gods of Data and benefited the bottom line. Trump began as Cecil the Lion, and then ended up president of the United States.

THIS PROFUSION OF DATA has changed the character of journalism. It has turned it into a commodity, something to be marketed, tested, and calibrated. Perhaps media have always thought this way. But if that impulse always existed, it was at least buffered. Magazines and newspapers used to think of themselves as something coherent—an issue, an edition, an institution. Not as the publisher of dozens of discrete pieces to be trafficked each day on Facebook, Twitter, and Google. The audience for journalism may be larger now, but the mind-set is smaller. Thinking about bundling articles into something larger was intellectually liberating. If readers didn't want a report on child poverty or a dispatch from South Sudan, it didn't matter. They wouldn't judge you for that. In fact, they might be flattered that you thought they might like to read such an article, even if they skipped right past it. Editors justified high-minded and quixotic articles as essential for the "mix."

Now assignments are subjected to a cost-benefit analysis—will the article earn enough traffic to justify the investment? This analysis is sometimes explicit and conscious, though often it's subconscious and embedded in euphemism. It's the train of thought that leads editors to declare an idea "not worth the effort" or to worry about how an article will "sink."

Journalism was vigilant about separating the church of editorial from the secular concerns of business. We can now see the justification for such fanaticism about building a thick, tall wall between the two. The fear was that we'd enter a world where readers couldn't tell the difference between editorial and advertising—where the corrupt hand of advertisers would interfere with the journalistic search for truth. Those fears are in the process of being realized.

The first breach in the barricade is something called "branded content" or "native advertising." These ads intend to solve the problem of Web advertising—all those banners atop Web pages have become highly ignorable din, ineffective means of branding a firm. Web banner ads physically sit on the fringes of editorial. Branded content is meant to be integrated into the very fabric of a Web site. It is an ad that is written to resemble journalism—a pseudo-piece about the new scientific consensus suggesting better ways to quit smoking in *Time*, or a sham article on the emerging workforce in the *New York Times*. Indeed, the ads are usually produced by the media companies themselves, not an ad agency. (The media companies often claim their staff of writers and editors have nothing to do with the copy, though typically it's their stable of freelancers who do the dirty work.) The wall isn't fully breached, however. There's usually a tag indicating that the article has been "sponsored" or "paid for by advertisers." But it's as discreet as possible, and that's the point. Advertisers will pay a premium for branded content, because it stands such a good chance of confusing the reader into clicking.

It seems scandalous that journalistic institutions would create a whole business based on misleading readers. But the scandal runs even deeper. Editorial increasingly resembles advertising. Many Internet publications write about companies and consumer goods with a breathlessness that resembles advertising. This isn't a coincidence. To sell ads, it helps to create an environment where advertisers feel assured that their message will be heard, or rather mistaken for editorial. BuzzFeed was the reductio ad absurdum of this. Very early in its life, it decided to make branded advertising its chief stream of revenue. To bolster this pursuit, it generated reams of stories that sounded just like press releases. Andrew Sullivan made sport of pointing this out. He ran a feature called "Guess Which BuzzFeed Piece Is an Ad." It was damn near impossible to detect any difference—"19 Incredible Things You Didn't Know About Dunkin' Donuts"; "The New iPhone Keyboard Changes Everything"; "The Only Post You Need to Read About the PlayStation 4." (Those were all supposedly legitimate works of journalism, not advertising.) How confused was Buzz-Feed about the difference between advertising and editorial? When writers published pieces critical of advertisers, BuzzFeed management vanished them from its site. (After public outcry, BuzzFeed conceded its sins and vowed not to repeat them.)

The relationship between advertiser and media is transformed. You can see the change in the language—"sponsor." Advertisers are no longer simply buying real estate to sell their products; they are acting as sort of beneficent patrons of journalism. Here we can see the stirrings of something far worse. It has become commonplace for journalistic organizations to recruit corporations and foundations as launch sponsors. Advertisers bankroll the debut of new journalistic products. One reason that an advertiser might play this role is perfectly harmless—it's good exposure. But there's another, more pernicious reason that they pay—the advertiser gets to play an opaque role in shaping the editorial product.

This was an approach we pursued at the *New Republic*. Chris Hughes recruited the billionaire activist Tom Steyer to pay hundreds of thousands for a new section of our Web site that would cover how climate change played in congressional elections—even as Steyer spent millions trying to influence those elections to elevate the issue of climate change. Chris also recruited Credit Suisse to pay for a new section of our Web site devoted to the future of banking, just as the bank tried to recover from accusations of tax evasion. The advertisers were trying to buy *New Republic* editorial to convey exactly their desired message, without readers having any sense of their massive infusions of cash. We shouldn't soften our description: This sort of arrangement is corrupt.

In the end, my colleagues and I managed to sabotage the

worst offenses. Steyer got so frustrated with our editorial staff that he decided to simply buy "sponsored content." Credit Suisse concluded that it was dangerous to pay a bunch of liberals to cover the future of banking; it ended up sponsoring a month's worth of articles about identity politics.

Defenders of native advertising have a point: It is hardly Armageddon. Radio announcers used to seamlessly shill for products as they went about reading the news. For decades, the *New York Times* editorial page included a regular piece of propaganda from Mobil Oil, clearly labeled but embedded among its prestige columnists.

The problem is that the relationship between advertisers and journalism has become so murky. Rules have relaxed, norms have changed. Until recently, the American Society of Magazine Editors was staunchly traditionalist, sternly forbidding journalists to touch ad copy. But in 2015, the guidelines softened. A once shrill condemnation is now a weak suggestion. "Editors should avoid working with and reporting on the same marketer." We need to understand these changes as dangerous surrenders. Advertisers are buying influence; they are buying the semblance of journalistic legitimacy; they are softening all the rules that bolster the integrity of the profession.

CHRIS HUGHES AND I ONCE sat at the breakfast table of an august Washington hotel pondering the core qualities of the *New Republic*—the *New Republic* that we would re-create together. We didn't ever say so explicitly, but we were searching for a piece of common ground, for an adjective that could unite everything we both wanted for the magazine. It felt like a roundabout exercise. If there was a whiteboard—and Chris loved whiteboards—it might be filled with discarded terms. But that rubbished verbiage was the futile prelude to a creative breakthrough. "We're idealistic," he said. "It ties together our storied past and our optimism about solutions." "Idealism" was a word that melted my heart, and I felt uncontainable joy at the prospect of agreement. "Boom. That's it."

We were idealistic about our shared idealism. Certain goals of ours overlapped. We both wanted the *New Republic* to thrive; we both believed in an activist vision of American government; we both believed in the importance of elevating the culture toward cosmopolitanism; we both loved the idea of long-form journalism. These similarities were enough for us to deceive ourselves into believing that we shared the same idealism.

Chris's vision of the world was essentially technocratic; mine was more moralistic and romantic. Where he liked the idea of long-form journalism, I ideologically believed in it. He believed in systems—rules, efficiencies, organizational charts, meetings, productivity tools. The world was eminently improvable, but progress requires escaping from overheated emotions and name-calling and excessive partisanship. This view of the world put him on a collision course with the politically committed intellectual free spirits who populated our office, who wrote with conviction and at odd hours, pursuing the subjects that gave them most satisfaction, not necessarily crowd-pleasing riffs.

Just before it all ended badly, Chris shared his revised vision of the magazine's future with me, the place to which his idealism had guided him. He had owned the *New Republic* for two years and he was getting antsy. Results, by which he meant greater Web traffic and greater revenue, needed to come faster. "To save the magazine, we need to change the magazine," he told me.

Engineers and marketers were going to begin playing a central role in the editorial process. They would give our journalism the "cool," "innovative" features that would make it popular, help it stand out in the marketplace. Of course, this required resources, and those resources would come from the pool that funded long-form journalism. I wasn't prepared for his plan or his description of the *New Republic*. "We're a technology company," he said. To which I responded, "That doesn't sound like the type of company that I'm qualified to run." He assured me that I could do the job.

Two months later I learned from a colleague that Chris had hired my replacement—and my replacement was lunching around New York offering jobs at the *New Republic*. Before Chris had the chance to fire me, I resigned, and nearly the whole editorial staff of the magazine quit, too. Their idealism dictated that they resist his idealism. They didn't want to work for a publication whose ethos more clearly aligned with the big tech companies than with journalism. They were willing to pay careful attention to Facebook, but didn't want their jobs defined by it. The bust-up received its fair share of attention and then faded—a road bump on Silicon Valley's route to engulfing journalism.

Eight

DEATH OF THE AUTHOR

SILICON VALLEY'S ASSAULT on journalism is a piece of a larger program. The technology companies want to overturn an entrenched idea at the heart of Western civilization. For three hundred years, our culture has venerated genius—it has made a fetish of originality and intellectual novelty. This can be a bit of an overwrought fixation. To state the banal, we know that there's no such thing as a wholly original idea. The intellectual life is never quite as solitary as it seems. But there were excellent reasons for buying into the cult of genius. We consider humanity capable of moral progress. Forward motion requires a constant infusion of new ideas, whose production we must lavishly credit to incentivize. We consider conformism to be spiritually and morally deadening, so we celebrate its opposite. Genius and originality were two of the most revelatory and lasting ideas to emerge from the intellectual revolutions of the eighteenth century.

Silicon Valley has an entirely different view of human creativity. It believes in the virtues of collaboration, that groups working harmoniously yield better ideas than the isolated individual. It considers originality to be a highly overrated ideal, even a pernicious one. By emphasizing genius, we allow a small cadre of professional writers to act as if they monopolize wisdom or possess some superhuman capabilities. The aura of genius surrounding the accomplished writer creates the impression that the masses have relatively little creative potential, which has justified force-feeding them the creative output of that small priesthood of geniuses.

If Silicon Valley were merely lampooning our old fetish for genius, that would be harmless, maybe even salutary. But its goals are far more revolutionary than that. It has set out to dismantle the structures that have protected our ideas of authorship. Silicon Valley has waged war on professional writers, attempting to weaken the copyright laws that make it possible for authors to make a living from their pen. It has pursued a business plan that radically deflates the value of knowledge, which renders writing a cheap, disposable commodity. To pull off this strategy, it has attempted to puncture the prestige of the professional author. This war is another instance of Silicon Valley's fake populism. Fittingly, its primary theorist is a Harvard law professor.

LONG BEFORE TED TALKS, there was Larry Lessig. His lectures and speeches were gripping spectacles of intellect, punctuated by multimedia. They became the stuff of legend. To this day, an official Microsoft tutorial provides lessons in how to give a "Lessig-style" talk. More than any other academic of his generation, Lessig has a feel for the zeitgeist. Before his fellow law professors had ever heard of the Internet, he made it his specialty. That doesn't quite give him enough credit: Lessig did more than study the Internet, he defended it against existential threats. One magazine profile described him as "a kind of Internet messiah."

What made this intellectual entrepreneurship so impressive was the seemingly narrow patch of academia from which Lessig launched himself. His nominal subject was the jurisprudence of copyright. But at an early date, he witnessed the entertainment industries' oppressive effort to criminalize the downloading of music, its campaign to cuff kids for the relatively innocent offense of file sharing. He thundered against these efforts with a passion that attracted hordes of followers.

While Lessig wrote about the niceties of the law, his real argument was about culture. Despite his elite pedigree—Oxbridge degree, Supreme Court clerkship—he formulated a case that was radical, borderline utopian. He wrote with wonderstruck lyricism. The Internet would change the means of cultural production, he argued. In the twentieth century, culture had been ripped from the people. It had been placed under the rule of avaricious corporations, which pumped out profitable dreck. The masses were reduced to mere consumers, passive couch-bound recipients of movies, television, and music produced in Los Angeles and New York. "Never before in the history of human culture had [creative culture] been as professionalized, never before as concentrated. Never before has the creativity of the millions been as effectively displaced." The Internet represented an opportunity to transcend that model, or rather, it could revive a very old one.

His argument went something like this: Once upon a time, people were active collaborators in the creation of culture. That was the essence of folk traditions. People took songs, tweaked them, and remade them as their own; they retold stories, adding their own embellishments. Higher forms of culture worked this way, too. What was Mark Twain but a skilled refashioner of the African American tales he overheard as a youth? If critics were honest, they would concede that every artist operated like this—borrowing, quoting, building supposedly original creations on the works of others. Jazz, at its core, entails the constant reinterpretation of the old songbook; hip-hop unapologetically swipes its beats and hooks. The great poets did this, too. T. S. Eliot, who stitched elusive and allusive quotations into his verse, issued the dictum "Immature poets imitate; mature poets steal."

Lessig gave Eliot's sentiment a cyber-age gloss. He described the difference between Hollywood's oppressive brand of "read-only culture" and the Internet's participatory "read-write culture." At the dawn of the Internet, these two cultures were engaged in nothing less than a civilizational war. The conglomerates, fearful of the threat the "read-write" culture posed to their businesses, wildly accused innocent civilians and idealistic tech companies of violating copyright laws. It was crucially important to thwart this campaign, Lessig wrote. "If communism vs. capitalism was the struggle of the twentieth century, then control vs. freedom will be the debate of the twenty-first century."

These arguments flew in the face of the culture's ingrained ideas of authorship. These ideas were embodied in the copyright laws that he wanted to dilute—and in the romantic ideas about writing that had been taught to schoolchildren over the centuries. The old ideas of authorship emphasized the import of originality. Western culture made plagiarism a punishable taboo; it frowned on derivative thinking as lazy.

The challenge to this antique idea of authorship didn't just emerge from Lessig. Indeed, some of the organizations that Lessig created to advance his arguments received checks from Google, which had its own reasons for promoting a critique of copyright. Most of Silicon Valley, however, agreed. During the early years of the Internet, theorists of technology aggressively celebrated amateurism. Elites had a chokehold on the country that prevented the masses from expressing their creativity. Clay Shirky described the pent-up genius as "cognitive surplus." The Internet helped unleash this surplus—it allowed bloggers to express the truths that careerist pundits dared not speak; citizen journalists scored new scoops; Wikipedia soon trumped *Britannica* with its depth and range. The amateurs could produce such brilliance because of the purity of their passion. As Shirky wrote: "Amateurs are sometimes separated from professionals by skill, but always by motivation; the term itself derives from the Latin *amare*—'to love.' The essence of amateurism is intrinsic motivation: to be an amateur is to do something for the love of it."

Our old idea of authorship romanticized the individual genius. It celebrated solitary toil at the desk as the highest form of creation. Silicon Valley championed a different theory of creativity. It emphasized the virtues of collaboration. Reid Hoffman, a cofounder of LinkedIn, enthused: "No one can succeed by themselves. . . . The only way you can achieve something magnificent is by working with other people." This could be seen in any number of Silicon Valley's favored terms: "peer production," "social media," "distributed knowledge." Wisdom could be found in the amassing of massive data sets, in analyzing the motion of markets. That is the essence of Google's ranking of Web sites, Amazon's recommendation algorithms, and Facebook's News Feed—all extrapolated from the accumulated wisdom of crowds.

There's a screaming irony to this view of creativity. It flies in the face of Silicon Valley's own creation myth. According to the story told about technology, and that technologists tell about themselves, creativity comes in the form of the fearless entrepreneur, the alienated geek working in the garage. This can sound a lot like Ayn Rand's view of heroic individuality, and may account for why so many technologists gravitate toward libertarianism. Rand's version of libertarianism also celebrates egotism. And there's something more than a bit egotistical in this view of culture. The titans of technology may be capable of breathtaking originality and solitary genius, but the rest of the world is not.

SILICON VALLEY'S VIEW OF CREATIVITY is medieval. Europe, in the era before the Enlightenment, didn't think much of authors. It also belittled originality, although for reasons that bear little resemblance to Lessig's case. All credit for creativity was due to the divine source of inspiration: "God alone creates," Thomas Aquinas asserted. Humans could produce only flawed imitations of the divine original.

Writers were dependent, fairly helpless creatures. They counted on the beneficence of royal and aristocratic patrons to finance the production of their work and to provide them with sustenance. Once a writer sold a manuscript, he surrendered control over it. It might be rewritten, lengthened, or mauled to pieces by a scribe or a printer. The writer had no choice but to submit to the butchering.

How little was originality valued? We now regard plagiarism as a grave intellectual sin, but the filching of words and plot ran rampant. Indeed, it was considered a primary tool of the craft. A good percentage of the body of work called Chaucer consists of translation and paraphrase. Shakespeare, for one, was a brilliant poet and an accomplished borrower. He lifted from Arthur

Brooke's *The Tragical History of Romeus and Juliet* and Plutarch's life of Mark Antony. "I am 'sort of' haunted by the conviction," Henry James wrote, "that the divine William is the biggest and most successful fraud ever practiced on a patient world." But if he was a plagiarist—and that's far too strong and unfair a term—it would have been impossible to level the charge against him. The word hadn't yet been coined.

As in Larry Lessig's utopia, culture was a collective effort; creation was guided by tradition. Cutting and pasting may have required a bit more effort than a click of a mouse, but it prevailed as a widespread method of creativity. We can be grateful that this mode of production yielded enduring monuments of culture, but it would be foolish to celebrate it as an ideal. There was a deep conservatism to the method. M. H. Abrams, the great cultural critic and literary historian, used the metaphor of the mirror to describe the mode. Writing wasn't meant to change the world; it aspired to reflect and mimic it. Copying was the natural ideal for a society that depended on obedience to crown and church, that stridently resisted change.

Technology, in the form of the printing press, helped shatter the mirror. The new machinery of type arrived with capitalism and the Enlightenment. That is, the printing press created the potential for mass production of the written word; capitalism created the potential for a mass market for the written word; and the Enlightenment created the political and intellectual space for writing to flourish. Scribes and copyists were suddenly vestigial figures; writers acquired a heroic cast. In part, this was the doing of book publishers. To stand out in a crowded market, you need to differentiate and hype your product. A book is more salable if it reflects the mind of a genius.

Writers—those formerly anonymous craftsmen, those cobblers of words—were suddenly pedestal-worthy. The crucial mythmaking figure was William Wordsworth. He was paid terribly for his work. With Samuel Coleridge, he split thirty pounds from the sale of their *Lyrical Ballads* (1798). This was hardly a fee fit for a genius—and that's what he considered the definition of true artistry. Wordsworth's aspirations were far grander than mirroring reality. In Wordsworth's view, a writer who merely recorded or re-created was a failure. Or in M. H. Abrams's formulation, writers were meant to be a lamp, incandescently projecting original insights into the world. Wordsworth wrote, "Of genius the only proof is, the act of doing well what is worthy to be done, and what was never done before. . . . Genius is the introduction of a new element into the intellectual universe."

Genius could flourish only with proper compensation—and that compensation would make sense only if the law protected the artist's work from pirates. (Because poets were rarely appreciated in their own time, copyright protections needed to be lengthy—so that there was enough time for the public's taste to catch up with genius.) Wordsworth spent decades lobbying for a substantial extension of copyright, created one hundred years earlier in the Statute of Anne. "Deny it to him, and you unfeelingly leave a weight upon his spirits, which must deaden his exertions; or you force him to turn his facilities . . . to inferior employments."

Wordsworth's case for copyright may very well have been self-interested and self-aggrandizing. But that's not very surprising. Originality demands arrogance. It's the hubristic faith that there are new ideas to be hatched, new forms to be invented. We need to accord originality higher status because the culture would gravitate toward banality and cliché if we didn't. Creating a new idea is risky because new ideas so often fall flat. The culture will always tend to repeat itself, to follow well-established formulas, because the safest way to make money and win popularity is to repeat the things that have worked before. Genius may be a bit of a sham, but it's a culturally important sham. To put it in terms that Silicon Valley might understand, we need to perpetuate the idea of genius because the idea breeds innovation. Of course, Silicon Valley could never accept such an analysis, because it would diminish its profits.

ROMANTICS IN GERMANY AND ENGLAND wrote about genius with the same rhetorical force as Wordsworth. So did the American Founding Fathers. But the Founders were imperfect protectors of authorship. They wrote copyright into the Constitution, but also left a yawning loophole. American law said nothing about the rights extended to foreign works. Bootleg copies of British books came to inundate the American market. The pirated editions were dirt cheap. A reader in London would have spent about $2.50 for a copy of Dickens's *A Christmas Carol*. On the other side of the Atlantic, the same volume sold for six cents. When books failed to sell in England, publishers shipped them to the giant remainder table that was the United States. It was a glut accentuated by the fierce competition among American printers. By 1830, ten houses in Philadelphia alone were churning out copies of Sir Walter Scott's work. As the publisher Henry Holt boasted, "[the] business lived to a large extent on what was morally, if not legally, thievery."

English authors would shake with rage at this condition. When Charles Dickens visited the United States in 1842, he spent his tour railing against American publishing. "I am the greatest loser by the existing Law, alive," he wailed. Rudyard Kipling, another big-time loser under the regime, placed a special order to a printer so that his complaints to an American publisher appeared on toilet paper: "Because you print the stolen property aforesaid very vilely and uncleanly, you shall be cursed from Alaska to Florida and back again."

This created a maddening paradox. Americans were highly literate, but American literature was highly peripheral. The canonical writers of the nineteenth century—who, sadly, never had the reputations they deserved in their lifetimes—depended on jobs in the customhouse, consulates, or other outposts of the civil service. (Political parties also provided steady gigs to scribes willing to pump out propaganda.) The great printers of the early Republic rarely put their muscle behind books. Despite the riches Ben Franklin reaped from his *Almanack*, he hardly printed any other volumes. When Walt Whitman wanted to publish *Leaves of Grass*, he was forced to assume the costs of printing himself.

Writing wasn't a profession. It was idealized as a hobby for patrician Men of Letters—who wanted to share their lifetime of erudition with the world and who considered compensation for their learned words to be vulgar. Henry Holt chided those who sought to dirty their noble words with talk of money. "Few men have ever [depended on their pen for income] happily. . . . Most good authors, from Shakespeare down, have had other resources. There are some pursuits in which it is almost as dangerous to make money the main end."

Mark Twain saw through this hokum. He became a leading champion of tightening the screws on American copyright. When he pressed the case, he unknowingly nodded to Kipling's protests.

"This country is being flooded with the best of English literature at prices which make a package of water closet paper seem an 'edition de luxe' in comparison." Publishers came to see the wisdom in his critique. Or more to the point, they were caught in a very ungentlemanly price war. Upstart firms flooded the market with cut-rate editions. After so many decades of seeing copyright legislation as inimical, publishers came to view it as a raft that would carry them back to the shores of profitability. In 1891, Congress heeded the plans of publishers and extended copyright to foreign works.

The law set in place a new economics, which transformed American writing from hobby to profession. This is the structure that the tech companies want to overturn. It's easy to get carried along by Facebook's arguments about sharing—and it's also easy to work up a lather over the media conglomerates that profit from ludicrous extensions of copyright laws. But it's important to remember how professionalization remade American letters: It democratized it. Writing became more diverse, more vibrant. This is counterintuitive. Professions are exclusionary; not everyone can earn a living from the pen. But the advent of book advances, magazine jobs, and hefty fees for writing assignments made writing a viable path for a far vaster population, who couldn't find the hours for such a consuming pastime. Almost immediately after Twain's triumph, writing was liberated from the privileged grasp of Brahmins.

For the first time in the history of the Republic, American literature came to dominate American tastes. A new generation of writers soon emerged, which better reflected the country, though very far from perfectly. It wasn't concentrated in any region or any caste. Jack London and Upton Sinclair came from poverty.

The hinterlands beyond New England and New York supplied writers like William Dean Howells, Theodore Dreiser, Ezra Pound, and Twain himself.

The sociology of American letters quickly changed because the economics did. Publishing became a big business. Writers produced the essential commodity, and their status and compensation came to reflect that fact. Magazines and newspapers had long neglected to credit the authors of pieces with a byline—that's how low they considered the scribes who supplied them with words. In these years, writers increasingly saw their names floating above their pieces, though the *New York Times* resisted that practice until the 1920s.

The sums that publishing conglomerates paid writers were suddenly quite impressive. William Dean Howells called himself a "theoretical socialist, and a practical aristocrat," though he confided to his father, "It is a comfort to be right theoretically and to be ashamed of one's self practically." (When calculated into present-day dollars, Howells took home $1,450,000 each year.) Or as Henry Holt sneered, "the golden goose was found for the author."

Bohemia may have been the romantic ideal—the movie set for the modern writer. But professionalism was the ethos. No matter the quantities of booze poured down the authorial gullet, the Protestant spirit of work prevailed. As with Taylorism in the factories, writers imposed quotas on themselves. Graham Greene raced to reach his five-hundred-word ceiling each morning. Ernest Hemingway squeezed the same from his drenched melon. Work, Hemingway declared, was "the one thing that always made you feel good." And despite his best efforts to squander his earnings, he left an estate worth $1.4 million. F. Scott Fitzgerald, who described himself as a "professional" with a "protective hardness," tracked his earnings in a ledger with an accountant's fastidious notations, even noting the $0.34 he received in 1929 for the English royalties of *The Great Gatsby*. (*Gatsby*, for the record, earned $8,397 in total royalties, and $18,910 when Fitzgerald peddled the movie rights.)

These quotidian details matter. Our great writers cared about money because they needed it. They needed it to feed their families, and so that they could devote themselves to fulfilling their creative selves. Without pay, they would have been consigned to day jobs, unable to fully apply themselves to their prose. Apologists for Amazon like to sneer at the writerly caste, a hermetic club that dismisses outsiders who aren't part of the gang. Yet history shows the alternative to professionalized writing. A few geniuses from the lower rungs of the class structure would manage to produce lasting art, despite the distant odds. But writing would largely survive as a luxury for those who could afford it, a hobby for the wealthy—for the trust fund babies, the men of leisure, those with the resources to follow their economically irrational passions.

YEARS AGO, I was working in the Houghton Library at Harvard, the hushed home to the magnificent contrails of American letters, the papers of Dickinson and Emerson and Theodore Roosevelt. My work done for the day, I had a few hours to spare and asked the librarians if I could have a look at the papers of the *New Republic*, which had been trucked to Cambridge over the decades. The collection hadn't been cataloged or sorted or even handled by an archivist. When it arrived at my table, it came in the form of old steel filing cabinets, wheeled by dollies. These towers soon crowded me, as if I were sitting in the middle of a museum version of the old office.

I began pulling drawers and disgorging files at random. As I settled the folders on the table, nervous about what my stubby fingers might inflict, I felt the fetishistic thrill of physically communing with greatness. Each page I turned over revealed the signature of canonical hands—air mail and postcards from Elizabeth Bishop, John Updike, Ralph Ellison, and Irving Howe. However glamorous the names of the correspondents, the content of the missives was strangely familiar to me. It precisely anticipated the email I received from writers. The files were filled with the eternal gripes: Why hadn't the check for the last piece arrived? Could the editor do any better with the fee? The letters were sometimes aggrieved, sometimes abject, rarely charming.

Staring at these artifacts, I thought of a passage in Alfred Kazin's memoir, *Starting Out in the Thirties*. As a young critic, Kazin would stop by the Chelsea offices of the *New Republic*'s literary editor, Malcolm Cowley. It was the bottom of the Depression. Writers queued for Cowley's attention. "There were just too many of us wedged onto the single bench in the waiting room downstairs," Kazin wrote. "Desperate cases haunting him for review[s]." The editor had a reputation for generosity with his assignments—which were like canned food from the church pantry that allowed writers to persist while their neighbors were famished.

That anecdote always seemed to me a reflection of that dark moment. But reading through the papers, I came to see that the sum Cowley paid was the disturbing revelation: $150 for a review. When I saw this figure in a letter, it gave me a stir. It was precisely the same amount the *New Republic* still paid for reviews of approximately the same length that we published on our Web site.

I stared at the page. Eighty years of inflation . . . and stagnation. Writers are still paid precisely the same sum they received at the lowest moment in the economic history of the modern world.

Over my time as a journalist, I've seen the proprietors of journalistic outfits come to the conclusion that writers don't really need to get paid very much. My career began at *Slate*, one of the first of the magazines created to live exclusively on the Internet. In those golden years, back in the midnineties, we paid one thousand dollars for each book review, and a few of our stars made even more than that. Today, *Slate* pays about three hundred dollars for a review.

We don't need to rely on anecdote. There are studies to be examined. In 1981, the Authors Guild surveyed its members. It found that full-time writers made a median income of about $11,000 per year—if we adjusted that sum for inflation, it would now be about $35,000. That doesn't sound like much at all, until we compare it with the Authors Guild's 2009 findings, which uncovered a median income of $25,000. Sadly, the number rolls further down the deflationary spiral. In 2015, the median income dropped to $17,500. Over thirty-four years, writers took a 50 percent pay cut. The present salary lurks not much higher than the government's official poverty line. Writing, a profession that once seemed fairly central to the project of Western civilization, is barely above water. The value of knowledge has been deflated and depressed, just as the tech companies intended.

EVERY MONTH, AS EDITOR, I would receive a report from our chief operating officer. In the parlance of modern business, it was a dashboard—a set of numbers and charts to keep tabs on the state of things. More precisely, the numbers tracked the productivity of my writers. The business gurus wanted me to think more rigorously and economically about our staff, to see precisely how many pieces they produced, the traffic garnered by those pieces, how writers performed on Facebook. Stated plainly on the dashboard: the salary and benefits paid to each writer, also the revenue that their articles generated for the business. (There was only one writer on staff who actually justified her salary, and it was because we paid her such a paltry sum.) They hoped that these numbers would guide me to increase the staff's productivity—to snap the whip a bit harder, to consider an axe blow to the traffic runts, to assign more clickable pieces.

I kept these dashboards under lock and key for fear of demoralizing the rest of the staff. They had already demoralized me. We had the best art critic in the world, a true shaper of taste, and the metrics showed only how few readers clicked on his pieces. Chris Hughes urged firing him, and goaded me to miraculously find a better return on our investment in his work. But there was no way to make him meaningfully more lucrative or quantifiably more "productive" without destroying his dedication to his craft, without gutting all the things that made him so great.

The problem was framed all wrong. If I had known better, I would have handed Chris a copy of an old book by the economists William Baumol and William Bowen called *Performing Arts: The Economic Dilemma*. The pair were interested in the economics of classical music. Turns out, a work like Beethoven's String Quartet No. 4 is a stubborn thing. When the piece debuted in Vienna, it took a full complement of musicians—two violins, one cello, and one viola. Two hundred years later, the performance of the piece hasn't changed a lick. It takes the same number of musicians, playing instruments that have hardly changed. As it did in 1801, the piece takes just about twenty-four minutes to complete. Classical music has, in other words, slapped classical economics in the face. Over the centuries, it hasn't become any more productive—and it can't.

The problem that Baumol and Bowen identified was subtler than that: They named a condition called "cost disease." While classical music hasn't grown any more productive, the cost of producing it keeps increasing. A symphony orchestra requires trained professionals. And if it hopes to recruit these professionals, it needs to pay them a salary that roughly competes with the rest of the economy, which grows progressively more expensive. (A passionate oboist will take a pay hit to pursue a love of music, but still needs enough to afford food, child care, and housing.) Without plausible pay, these musicians will choose some other, more viable line of work.

Classical music has been in a state of terminal decline for decades. Cost disease is at the heart of this decay. It's the reason that a concert ticket feels like a major philanthropic commitment—and why the middle class can't afford an active interest in the genre. It's the reason that arts organizations are perpetually sitting on the edge of financial collapse.

Writing is a bit different from classical music. For starters, it involves the creation of new work, not just the repetition and reinterpretation of a repertoire. There are always fresh goods to take to market. Growth is, therefore, not a quixotic quest. Besides, publishing seems to always find ways to grab a little productivity here and there. It can move printing presses to Asia; it can use technology to speed the process of assembling a book; it can sell e-books that cull the cost of cloth, paper, and distibution; its firms will merge to reduce back-office costs.

Yet there's really no shortening the time it takes to write a book or a magazine article of substance—and there's nothing that can be done to change that without changing the fundamental nature of the enterprise. No penny-pinching technology can remove the human from the fundamental process of creation, no piece of software can speed the production of thought, even as the cost of producing books gallops ahead with the rest of the economy.

For many centuries, publishers lived in denial of cost disease. In fact, they spent large parts of their day in denial of the fact that they worked for fully capitalist enterprises. Over time, they rationalized their firms—they attempted to master the sciences of marketing and supply-chain management. Yet there was a fundamental mystery at the heart of book publishing. It was impossible to know the worth of a book before its publication, no way to predict its value with any precision. Each book is its own entity, its own fickle market. What's more, the denizens of publishing houses didn't necessarily approach their jobs with a mercantilist mind-set. The editors who presided over publishing considered themselves tastemakers, artists in their own right. Jason Epstein, one of the great editors of the last century, wrote, "Trade book publishing is by nature a cottage industry, decentralized, improvisational, personal; best performed by small groups of like-minded people, devoted to their craft, jealous of their autonomy, sensitive to the needs of writers and to the diverse interests of readers. If money were their primary goal, these people would probably have chosen other careers." Really, they were heirs to the old feudal tradition of patronage. That tradition never quite disappeared, and publishers felt obligations to the culture and to posterity. Somehow, they created a business that worked in spite of itself. They managed to produce enough hits to sustain the publication of works with negligible profits.

Amazon, however, has tattered that view of authorship. With its market share, publishers are utterly dependent on the Bezos behemoth to sell their product. This gives Amazon the power to squeeze and further squeeze its suppliers, to dictate terms to publishers. Its contracts with publishers extract capricious fees and far larger chunks of profit than a more competitive marketplace would demand. Publishers have acquiesced to Amazon at times, and violently resisted at others. Yet there's no real recourse. When Amazon tightens its chokehold around publishers, it is authors who suffer. The houses shrink the number of titles they publish; they carve the advances they pay to authors into smaller chunks, doled out over larger spans of time. We can hardly ascribe the collapse in author pay to Amazon alone, but it has become a primary driver of the deflation of writing. Facebook and Google have found an even more effective cure for writing's cost disease. They never, ever, under any circumstances, pay for it.

WRITING AS A PROFESSION is slowly decaying. We've been led by the hand to the brink by wild-eyed enthusiasts, like Chris Anderson, one of the Valley's most esteemed thinkers:

> In the past, the media was a full-time job. But maybe the media is going to be a part time job. Maybe media won't be a job at all, but will instead be a hobby. There is no law that

says that industries have to remain at any given size. Once there were blacksmiths and there were steel workers, but things change. The question is not should journalists have jobs. The question is can people get the information they want, the way they want it? The marketplace will sort this out. If we continue to add value to the Internet we'll find a way to make money. But not everything we do has to make money.

History has supplied some pretty definitive examples that undermine Anderson's euphoric theory. During the first decade of this century, blogging flowered. Amateurs wrote with joy and what seemed like boundless energy. Many pundits were overawed by this effusion, and they came to view the whole caste of professional writers as superfluous, inferior even. Ten years later, those predictions about the triumph of the bloggers look fairly delusional. The army of amateur bloggers had moments of brilliance, but it wasn't sustainable brilliance. Their ranks have diminished; the blogging moment has largely passed.

Over the centuries, writing became a profession, because it demands the discipline of a professional. There are only so many hours in the day for amateur pursuits—and very few writers are as gifted as Wallace Stevens or T. S. Eliot or Sylvia Plath, able to generate something lasting from stolen moments. Writing requires revision, fruitless hours of staring at screens, painstaking research. The flawed assumption in Anderson's prediction was that the joyous production of knowledge was enough to fuel writers through a lifetime of tough moments. Like everyone else, writers dedicate themselves to their job for a variety of reasons, but those reasons include paying the bills.

When writing was professionalized in the late nineteenth century, the culture deepened. Writers began producing investigative journalism, novels of ideas, reported magazine features—complex, labor-intensive genres that require full mental devotion, the sort of devotion that we associate with a job. With professionalism, writers began to develop expertise. They operated under codes of conduct that held their work to a high standard of ethics. They began to take intellectual risks, because their profession rewarded risks—with more lucrative jobs and Pulitzer Prizes and National Book Awards.

But let's not dwell in the irretrievable past, Silicon Valley instructs. Romantic authorship is dead and a glorious future awaits. Kevin Kelly has seen it. From his perch at *Wired* magazine, which he cofounded, he has produced an imposing oeuvre of futurism. With his gray Amish beard, Kelly has a prophetic visage and a prose style to match, passionately intense and full of grandiose pronouncements. He writes lines of homily, which end in rousing perorations: "Greater technology will selfishly unleash our talents, but it will also unselfishly unleash others: our children, and all children to come."

When Google began scanning every book on the planet, Kelly wrote one of the signature essays of the age, published by the *New York Times Magazine*. He considered Google's ambitions audacious, so audacious that it couldn't fully comprehend the implications of its program. Kelly, however, could discern them. The book was an ancient technology, and it was being profoundly disrupted by technology. Change would come imperceptibly, as the book slipped from the control of authors and publishers. Readers would seize the prerogative, exploiting technology to rework books to make them their own, mashing books into a new genre, something like Wikipedia pages. "The real magic will come in the second act, as each word in each book is cross-linked, clustered, cited, extracted, indexed, analyzed, annotated, remixed, reassembled and woven deeper into the culture than ever before."

It was the type of dream that McLuhan or Brand might have conjured. The network—the global community united by technology—would begin to melt the differences that separate us. One book would begin to dissolve into the next; copying and pasting and borrowing would blur all the distinctions that had once defined volumes. "In a curious way, the universal library becomes one very, very, very large single text: the world's only book." It was, as he admitted with his own choice of rhetoric, a religious dream. He described the future as the "Eden of everything." There was a political corollary to this prelapsarian dream. Not only would volumes melt into one beautiful book, disagreements would fade, too. (This was Leibniz's vision, revised and updated.) As readers worked together to annotate and edit texts, they would find common ground. The path of the network takes our most contentious debates and leads them toward consensus. Facebook puts it this way: "By enabling people from diverse backgrounds to easily connect and share their ideas, we can decrease world conflict in the short and long term."

But we know this is an illusion. Facebook leads us to a destination that is the precise opposite of its proclaimed ideal. It creates a condition that Eli Pariser has called the "Filter Bubble." Facebook's algorithms supply us with the material that we like to read and will feel moved to share. It's not hard to see the intellectual and political perils of this impulse. The algorithms unwittingly supply readers with texts and videos that merely confirm deeply felt beliefs and biases; the algorithms suppress contrary opinions that might agitate a user. Liberals are deluged with liberal opinions; vegetarians are presented with endless vegetarian agitprop; the alt-right is fed alt-right garbage; and so on. Facebook shields us from the sort of challenging disagreement—although not from the idiocy of trolls and the blather of comments sections—that might change our minds or help us to better understand the views of our fellow citizens.

In economics, the peril of the network is monopoly—where a competitive market comes under the sway of big corporations. In culture, the peril of the network is conformism—where a competitive marketplace of ideas ceases to be so competitive, where the emphasis shifts to consensus. Kevin Kelly, in his enthusiasm, unwittingly conveyed the darker implications of his vision. He extolled the "hive mind"—which is what happens when we get past our fetish for the author and give in to crowdsourcing and wikis and the hordelike tendencies of social media, when we surrender ourselves to the wise crowd. The hive mind was meant to describe a thing of beauty, humanity working in gorgeous concert. But really, who would want to live in a hive? We know from history that this sort of consensus is a plastic beauty, a stifling sameness. It deadens disagreement, strangles originality.

This is true of our politics. Our era is defined by polarization, warring ideological gangs that yield no ground. Division, however, isn't the root cause of our unworkable system. There are many causes, but a primary problem is conformism. Facebook has created two hive minds—the hive always has a queen bee—each residing in an ecosystem that nurtures head-nodding agreement and penalizes dissenting views. A hive mind is an intellectually incapacitated one, with diminishing ability to sort fact from fiction, with a bias toward evidence that confirms the party line. Facebook has managed to achieve consensus, but not quite as it promised. Instead of drawing the world together, the power of its network has helped tear it apart. Say all the ill things that can be said about our old ideas of genius and originality— none are worse than this.

SECTION III

TAKE BACK
THE MIND

Nine

IN SEARCH OF
THE ANGEL OF DATA

IN THE MIDDLE OF THE LAST CENTURY, the tech companies wouldn't have had the run of the field. They would have been closely watched and occasionally leashed. Americans knew better how to deal with big corporations and their dangers—or at least they cared about the problem then. The ills of monopoly were a feature of political rhetoric and a bipartisan priority of government, especially when companies played an outsized role in the transmission of ideas and knowledge.

Economic concentration has tumbled as a concern since then. In part, this reflects a changing consensus about the government's role, a long turn toward the light footprint preached by the libertarians and neoclassical economists at the University of Chicago. But the tech monopolies also represent something novel in the history of American business. To manage the threat, government needs a dramatic updating, a bolder program for regulating the Internet, a whole new apparatus for protecting privacy and the competitive marketplace. But before we can redress the problem, we need to be precise about it and to understand its genesis.

In 1989, the Berlin Wall piled into collectible rubble—and the Internet was born in its modern form. The events were spiritually tethered. That idealistic year, capitalism shed its historic competitor, and the Internet began its own journey to the free market.

The American government nurtured the nascent Internet— the "inter-network" in the geeked-out parlance of its earliest days. In the 1960s, the Defense Department supplied the grants to start it, to build a communications system that could withstand a Soviet assault. When it no longer made sense for the Pentagon to manage the system, which had strayed unrecognizably from its original militaristic purpose, the Defense Department handed control over to the National Science Foundation, another corner of the bureaucracy. Government stewards imposed strict controls on the Internet, forbidding "extensive use for private or personal business."

State supervision of the Internet worked well enough, but the National Science Foundation administrators were farseeing. They understood that the government shouldn't manage its potent creation. Just as the world took a neoliberal turn, the National Science Foundation conceived a multiyear plan for privatizing the Internet. Without the shackles of the state, the Internet would realize its revolutionary potential as an engine of global commerce and mass communication. If the planet was gliding toward the End of History, a globalized, liberal order, then the Internet was going to carry it all the way toward that glorious resting point.

The euphoria of capitalism's triumph set the tone for the Internet's emergence. Time-honored strands of wisdom seemed no longer relevant. Through the twentieth century, the governments of the Western world had imposed rules on the private sector—regulations to limit the harm that business and finance might inflict on the common good. But history seemed to be arcing away from that approach. The Soviet failure cast suspicion on statist solutions. So, the government didn't just privatize the Internet; it self-consciously decided that it would allow it to grow with hardly any government supervision. "I want to create an oasis from regulation in the broadband world," William Kennard, the chairman of the Federal Communications Commission, declared in 1999, mouthing a familiar sentiment.

For a time, the Internet lived the dream of 1989. The privatization of the Internet might even be one of capitalism's most glorious successes, though government played its role, too. Antitrust cases dogged IBM and AT&T into the eighties. The giants were too hobbled, too fearful of antagonizing Justice Department lawyers, to seize control of the Internet at the crucial moment of opportunity. It was a stroke of serendipitous timing, as well as shrewd bureaucratic planning. The Internet wasn't captured by a single firm. These conditions gave rise to a glorious festival of creative destruction. New companies rose and then fell, innovation exploded in all directions, inaccessible troves of knowledge were instantly available, a consumer's Arcadia emerged.

It was widely assumed that the history of business settled into a new pattern, what boosters called the New Economy. Firms would never achieve long-lasting dominance in the era of the Internet. Indeed, six years after the last phase of privatization, an astonishing percentage of the highly valued firms spiraled to their doom, in the inglorious dot-com crash. It didn't matter whether these companies affixed their names to sports stadiums or whether they had just begun to revolutionize commerce. One of history's great busts wiped them out. The market's stiletto puncture set our view of the Internet: The Web would never settle into a static pattern. No firm could avoid the patricidal fate of being done in by some young savant in a garage. The Web fostered the conditions for perfect competition, as if an economics professor had designed it. Consumers could always flee to the cheaper alternative or effortlessly shift to the better technology. As the wisdom held, "competition is always just a click away."

This has proved a wishful view, although for an astonishingly long stretch it held. The era of openness and flux has drawn to a close, inevitably. In his history of communications, Tim Wu described a progression of capitalism that he called The Cycle. Each new information technology follows the same trajectory: "From somebody's hobby to somebody's industry; from jury-rigged contraption to slick production marvel; from a freely accessible channel to one strictly controlled by a single corporation or cartel." History hasn't perfectly repeated itself, but we've reached the hardened end of Wu's cycle. We need to entertain the possibility that the monopolies of our day may be even more firmly entrenched than the giants in whose path they stride. One of the reasons for the growing distance between the tech companies and their competition is that they have such a large stockpile of a precious asset.

ONE OF THE CLICHÉS OF OUR TIME: *Data is the new oil*. This felt like hyperbole when first articulated, but now feels perfectly apt. "Data" is a bloodless word, but what it represents is hardly bloodless. It's the record of our actions: what we read, what we watch, where we travel over the course of a day, what we purchase, our correspondence, our search inquiries, the thoughts we begin to type and then delete. With enough data, it is possible to see correlations and find patterns. The computer security guru Bruce Schneier has written, "The accumulated data can probably paint a better picture of how you spend your time, because it doesn't have to rely on human memory." Data amounts to an understanding of users, a portrait of our psyche. Eric Schmidt once bragged, "We know where you are. We know where you've been. We can more or less know what you're thinking about."

A portrait of a psyche is a powerful thing. It allows companies to predict our behavior and anticipate our wants. With data, it is possible to know where you will be tomorrow within twenty meters and to predict, with reasonable accuracy, whether your romantic relationship will last. Capitalism has always dreamed of activating the desire to consume, the ability to tap the human brain to stimulate its desire for products that it never contemplated needing. Data helps achieve this old dream. It makes us more malleable, easier to addict, prone to nudging. It's the reason that Amazon recommendations for your next purchase so often result in sales, or why Google ads result in clicks.

The dominant firms are the ones that have amassed the most complete portraits of us. They have tracked us most extensively as we travel across the Internet, and they have the computing power required to interpret our travels. This advantage becomes everything, and it compounds over time. Bottomless pools of data are required to create machines that effectively learn—and only these megacorporations have those pools of data. In all likelihood, no rival to Google will ever be able to match its search results, because no challenger will ever be able to match its historical record of searches or the compilation of patterns it has uncovered.

In this way, data is unlike oil. Oil is a finite resource; data is infinitely renewable. It continuously allows the new monopolists to conduct experiments to master the anticipation of trends, to better understand customers, to build superior algorithms. Before he went to Google, as the company's chief economist, Hal Varian cowrote an essential handbook called *Information Rules*. Varian predicted that data would exaggerate the workings of the market. "Positive feedback makes the strong get stronger and the weak get weaker, leading to extreme outcomes." One of these extreme outcomes is the proliferation of data-driven monopolies.

It's a disturbing convergence: These companies have become dominant on the basis of their extensive surveillance of users, the total monitoring of activities, their ever-growing dossiers—what Maurice Stucke and Ariel Ezrachi call "a God-like view of the marketplace." Put bluntly, they have built their empires by pulverizing privacy; they will further ensconce themselves by continuing to push boundaries, by taking even more invasive steps that build toward an even more complete portrait of us. Indeed, the threats to privacy and the competitive marketplace are now one and the same. The problem of monopoly has changed shape.

THOUGH IT'S DIFFICULT TO IMAGINE from the vantage of the present, the issue of monopoly dominated our politics for generations. The underlying questions in the debate cut to the core of the Republic: We feared concentrations of corporate power would inhibit freedom and make a mockery of democracy. Those anxieties remain, though the debate on monopoly has grown ever more narrow. Antitrust law—the body of laws designed to preserve a competitive economy—has grown so technical and morally desiccated that it has little to say about the dominant firms of our own time, companies that would have represented the sum of all the old anxieties about gigantism. We need to return to the spirit of those original laws, but we have spent decades veering in the other direction.

The hinge figure in this narrative—the crucial player at the moment when the fight against monopoly surrendered its rhetoric of righteousness—was a cowboy in nearly every sense. He came from Laramie, Wyoming, back when the West was exotic and unimaginably distant, though his blazing wit and acerbic humor won him a fixed place in the American Establishment. Thurman Arnold taught at Yale Law in the 1930s and wrote with misanthropic flair. His signature work, *The Folklore of Capitalism*, was heavily indebted to the acidic critic of the "Booboisie," H. L. Mencken. The book was a precise account of all the illusions that prevailed in American life, described with clinical (and satirical) detachment as if Arnold were a "man from Mars." Our institutions, he argued, maintain their legitimacy because they are bolstered by lies. His assessment of the American people was so dim that he preferred these cynical fibs to actual democracy, what he described as "the feeble judgment of the common herd." Among our empty rituals and "popular moral gestures": antitrust laws. These laws were emotionally satisfying but did nothing to stall economic concentration.

It was especially odd, therefore, that Franklin Roosevelt appointed Arnold to head the Justice Department's Antitrust Division in 1938. His confirmation hearings were an especially uncomfortable affair. Arnold, who could be quite suave, would later admit that he struggled mightily to find a convincing explanation that could square his critique of antitrust law with his deep desire for the job. He was grilled by William Borah of Idaho, a target of his book: "Men like Senator Borah founded political careers on the continuance of such crusades, which were entirely futile but enormously picturesque." Still, that was a more deferential, more forgiving era. The Senate confirmed Arnold, although Borah allowed that Arnold should "revise that chapter on trusts."

As it turned out, Arnold did his job with incredible vigor. The Antitrust Division had been moribund when he arrived. On average, it filed nine suits a year. In 1940, once Arnold gathered a head of steam, he prosecuted ninety-two companies. His targets were scattered across the American economy, everywhere really: the motion picture industry, dairy, newsprint, and transportation. The war prematurely aborted his efforts. But never before, and never since, has the government more aggressively enforced antitrust laws. Consider where we now stand: The Obama administration brought two cases to bust up existing monopolies.

Even if his successors weren't as active as Arnold, they accepted his thinking. True to the steely realism in his writing, Arnold stripped antitrust law of its grand, rhetorical ambitions. The intellectual godfathers of Progressive Era antitrust law—men like Supreme Court Justice Louis Brandeis and President Woodrow Wilson—presented themselves as heirs to Thomas Jefferson. They hated corporate bigness because they viewed it as a threat to self-government. In their view, the protagonists of history were the small shopkeepers and small producers—or as Wilson called them, "men who are on the make." Economic independence equipped them for the duties of citizenship, an independence that the monopolies stomped.

Arnold considered this obsession with civic virtue a piece of garbage—a strain of "old religion." He couldn't have cared less about the size of a business, or even the fact of its monopoly. Brandeis considered "bigness" to be a "curse"; Arnold didn't. "That debate is like arguing whether tall buildings are better than low ones, or big pieces of coal better than small ones," Arnold wrote. In Arnold's view, antitrust law had one mission, and one mission alone: It needed to prosecute industries that were inefficient and whose inefficiency injured the welfare of consumers. As the political theorist Michael Sandel has written, "Unlike antimonopolists in the tradition of Brandeis, Arnold sought not to decentralize the economy for the sake of self-government but to regulate the economy for the sake of lower consumer prices."

Arnold's line of thinking has prevailed through the present. We begin to worry about economic concentration only when it is achieved through big mergers or through nefarious tactics. And we begin to fret about a firm's dominance only when it jacks up prices. Which is to say, we almost never take action that might dislodge an incumbent monopoly. The concentration of economic power is an accepted fact of our lives. When the *Economist* analyzed the question last year, it found that most sectors of the economy—two-thirds of the nine hundred areas it examined—were far more concentrated than they were in 1997. The Roosevelt Institute has declared, "markets are now more concentrated and less competitive than at any point since the Gilded Age."

The old obsession with the consumer was narrow, but it wasn't misguided. The economy, however, has morphed considerably since Arnold's day. Some of the biggest corporations in America now give their products away for free; Amazon and Walmart may not hand out freebies, but they are maniacal about low prices. By Arnold's standard, there's not much to fear about these behemoths. Perhaps we should worry about how they squelch competitors, but there's little reason to fret about the inefficiency of these industries. That, however, is a fairly incomplete view of the role these companies play in American life. Arnold's vision of antitrust law remains relevant, but the problem of monopoly in our time more closely tracks the nightmare scenario described by Brandeis. The threat of bigness posed by Amazon, Facebook, and Google is a threat to self-government.

BRANDEIS—THE CORPORATE LAWYER turned corporate scourge—could be a prude and a scold, neither of which negates the power of his opinions. His great concern was the quality of democracy. He really meant the quality of its citizens. Deep strains of populism and snobbery coexisted in his view of his fellow Americans. The populist in him believed in the limitless potential of everyday people to formulate sophisticated, well-reasoned opinions. As a snob, he disdained how citizens were seduced by the lure of consumerism and spun around by advertising. The potential of the average American could be fulfilled only with reading, contemplation, and extensive engagement with the higher forms of culture. When he spoke about the subject, he would passionately point to the need for workers and shopkeepers to "develop their faculties."

All these exhortations about contemplation and reading weren't just intended as a form of self-help. They were cornerstones of his political philosophy, which he later developed in the rulings he issued as a Supreme Court justice: "The final end of the State was to make men free to develop their faculties." He formulated and then reformulated our modern understanding of privacy in order to create the conditions for men and women to think independently and critically. The legal scholar Neil Richards has described Brandeis's theory as "intellectual privacy"—"the protection from surveillance or interference when we are engaged in the processes of generating ideas." Public debate was possible only after the formulation of private opinions—and that required the freedom to experiment and discard ideas, without worrying about prying eyes. If we believe we're being watched, we're far less likely to let our minds roam toward opinions that require courage or might take us beyond the bounds of acceptable opinion. We begin to bend our opinions to please our observer. Without the private space to think freely, the mind deadens—and then so does the Republic. Brandeis wrote, "The greatest menace to freedom is an inert people."

There were crucial assumptions in Brandeis's thinking that demand revival. The first was a critique of efficiency. It's not that Brandeis entirely rejected the idea. He was a devoted student of Frederick Taylor, the apostle of scientific management who used stopwatches and data-driven methods to make factories churn at a faster clip. But Brandeis hated the prospect that society might elevate efficiency to the highest value. Convenience was nice, but we shouldn't sacrifice ourselves to achieve it. His fear was that the benefits of efficiency might lure us to surrender our liberty. That's the authoritarian temptation: that liberty comes to seem a small price for trains that run on time. To update the thought—it's not worth having free email if the price is our privacy; next-day delivery is nice, but not if the consequence is a sole company dominating retail, setting the market price for goods and labor.

A second assumption flowed from the first. The Framers preferred liberty to efficiency, which is why they designed a less than efficient form of government. They checked, they balanced, intentionally slowing the machinery of the state they designed. Brandeis believed in the importance of countervailing powers. Democracy struggles for breath when one realm of society becomes too big and powerful. He believed that unions were necessary for limiting the power of corporations. And that oligopoly was such an imminent danger to the Republic that the state could take drastic action to prevent that condition. Not that Brandeis fully trusted the state—rather, he preferred to keep power devolved to units smaller and less menacing than the federal government. But in his view of modern life, the primary fear—which remains as terrifying as ever—was that a small group of companies would achieve outsized political and economic power. "The American people have as little need of oligarchy in business as in politics," he wrote.

There's no doubting what Brandeis would have made of Google, Facebook, and Amazon, which embody the full collection of his fears. They are monopolies operating without restraint, regulatory or otherwise. The companies preach the gospel of efficiency as they engage in the most extensive surveillance in human history. They are rent-seekers with little regard for the independent producers whose goods they sell. They shape the minds of citizens, filtering the information by which citizens arrive at their political opinions. Brandeis helped set the norms for modern American life, and the companies have built the systems that grievously injure those norms.

IN BRANDEIS'S DAY, the case for regulation rallied the masses. In our day, we can't quite see anything wrong with monopoly, especially not when it comes to these companies. We're certain that our tech giants achieved their dominance fairly and squarely through the free market, by dint of technical genius. To conjure this image of meritocratic triumph requires overlooking several pungent truths about the nature of these new monopolies. Their dominance is less than pure. They owe their dominance to innovation, but also to tax avoidance. Of course, every big American corporation tries to limit the tax bill. Armies of accountants are a staple of capitalism; the manufacture of new deductions is one of our country's greatest showcases of innovation. But the tech companies are especially slippery with the tax man. In part, it's the nature of their product. Unlike manufacturing or finance, tech doesn't need to be pinned to a geographic home. Tech companies can transfer their core assets, their intellectual property, to whatever tax haven offers the sweetest deal. They have hatched schemes that their competitors—brick-and-mortar firms, media companies—couldn't dare attempt.

When Jeff Bezos first conceived of Amazon, he originally wanted to locate the company on a California Indian reservation, where it would pay hardly any tax. Authorities rejected that gambit. But Bezos understood that Internet commerce challenged traditional ideas about taxation. Thanks to a court ruling, rendered just as he launched his company, Amazon could get away without paying sales tax to the states to which it shipped its goods.

But as the company expanded, it needed employees spread across the country. Each time Amazon opened a warehouse in a different state, it should have paid taxes there—at least that was the prevailing understanding of the law. Bezos rejected it. There was something Nixonian about this effort. Traveling Amazon employees carried misleading business cards, so that the company couldn't be accused of operating in a state. When Amazon opened a warehouse in Texas, the company apparently didn't tell the state tax officials about the building. That's a hard secret to keep. After authorities read an exposé in the *Dallas Morning News*, Bezos vowed not to pay the $269 million the company owed. If the state wanted that cash, he would shut down his facility and take his business elsewhere. In the end, Texas forgave Amazon's debts, so long as it accounted for itself honestly in the future. Texas was a template for the nation. When Amazon moved into South Carolina, the company finagled a five-year exemption from sales tax as a precondition for building a distribution center there.

Amazon promised the cheapest prices—and delivered that to consumers. It could offer the best price only by resisting tax. Economists at Ohio State University have shown the crucial role that avoidance played in establishing Amazon. They studied Amazon's sales after states ultimately forced it to pay tax. When states began collecting, household spending at Amazon dropped by 10 percent. In his history of Amazon, the journalist Brad Stone described this dodging as "one of the company's biggest tactical advantages."

Avoiding tax is an overriding corporate obsession—"employing every trick in the book, and inventing many new ones" in Stone's words. To outmaneuver the IRS and European collectors, Amazon hatched Project Goldcrest. The code name referenced the national bird of Luxembourg. In 2003, the company sought out a deal with the Grand Duchy. As a reward for building a headquarters there, it would pay hardly any tax. Once Amazon set up shop in Luxembourg, it transferred a vast swath of its intangible assets there—vital software, trademarks, and other shards of intellectual property. Truly, these assets exist in no particular country—does one-click shopping really have a physical location?—but they have a basis in contracts, and those contracts are the basis for taxation. Amazon devised a labyrinthine corporate structure, a dizzying network of subsidiaries and holding companies. As Amazon relocated, it drastically understated the value of the assets it shifted to Luxembourg. The whole plot has irked the IRS, which has built a careful case against Amazon. Calculations by the IRS show that Project Goldcrest helped Amazon to dodge a bill of at least $1.5 billion that would otherwise have been paid to the U.S. government.

Google has the same sort of unpatriotic accounting schemes. It prefers maneuvers known as the Double Irish and the Dutch Sandwich. Google has also shifted assets to Bermuda, that famous mecca of high tech. By the end of 2015, it had "permanently reinvested" $58.3 billion of its profits in foreign tax havens, earnings on which it pays no U.S. tax. The tech companies maintain every shred of data, yet seem to want to purge every bit of taxable earnings. The year Facebook went public, it recorded $1.1 billion in American profits, but didn't pay a cent of federal or state income tax. Indeed, it earned a $429 million refund. According to Citizens for Tax Justice, Facebook bilked the treasury by taking a single deduction: It wrote off the stock options it gave to its executives.

It's hard to have sympathy with Walmart or Home Depot or the other big-box stores. They hardly pay the largest tax rates in the nation. Still, they cough up a reasonable sum. Over the last decade, Walmart, the supposed Beast of Bentonville, handed over about 30 percent of its income in taxes; Home Depot paid 38 percent. We can bemoan the fact that they don't pay more, yet it seems reasonable to note that their prime competitor isn't paying even half that rate. Amazon averaged an effective tax rate of 13 percent—that includes taxes owed to states and localities, as well as the feds and foreign governments. Apple and Alphabet were only slightly less adventurous with their avoidance. They both paid a rate of about 16 percent. This is one of the dangers of monopoly that caused Brandeis such agita. Our biggest companies manage to acquire power, a sense of impunity, that allows them to further extend their advantages, to further shirk their public responsibilities.

These companies can afford to push the limits of acceptable behavior, because they have paid such care and attention to Washington. While the tech companies are hardly the image of corpulent K Street, they have built massive lobbying operations that pace the halls of the regulatory agencies and Congress, stacked with skillful hacks. Google executives set foot in the Obama White House more often than those of any other corporation—its head lobbyist visited 128 times. Google spread its money across Washington with joyous ecumenicism. Google spent about $17 million on influence peddlers of both partisan varietals. By one count, Google poured more into its D.C. apparatus than any other public company. An investigation by *The Intercept* concluded: "Google has achieved a kind of vertical integration with the government." Somehow Google managed to overcome the recommendation of staffers on the Federal Trade Commission who found Google's monopolistic machinations worthy of a lawsuit.

Lobbyists for the companies have preserved a blissful state of barely regulated, barely taxed monopoly. They have played the politics brilliantly. Obama spent his presidency cheering on the tech companies, even pleading with the Europeans not to collect the taxes owed to them. In return, the tech companies have sent their best brains to work for the Democratic administration and its political campaigns. The tech monopolists have aligned themselves with the left, culturally and electorally, which has defanged their most likely critics. That's the wise way to hedge: Republicans might not especially care for the donations that the tech companies send to Democrats, but they have no ideological interest in placing them under the thumb of government. Big tech has created a corporate paradise, which will prevail, until it doesn't.

THE TECH COMPANIES have so mastered Washington, they have acquired such cultural prestige, that it's hard to imagine the system ever restraining them. But we know that politics doesn't repose in a steady state, and the companies have one gaping vulnerability—they aggressively surveil users. Thus far, the public has tolerated these invasions, but that won't last forever.

Hackers are constantly testing security cordons, and constantly bursting through them. Everybody has tolerated this as a fact of digital life, a minor price to pay for its wonders. With the exception of Russian interference in our election, these have been relatively minor breaches. They will prove throat clearing compared with the Big One, the inevitable mega-hack that will rumble society to its core. The Big One might be an exposed cache of intimate information that disrupts marital relations en masse, as the Ashley Madison hack did on a small scale. It might disrupt our financial system, so that fortunes disappear in an unrecoverable flash. Or it might trigger an actual explosion of infrastructure that kills. If we could predict, we could prevent, but we can't.

The tech companies can see the Big One coming, and they

are bracing for the fallout, which is a perfectly reasonable posture. Their companies have created devices and code that enable omnipresent surveillance; their pack-rat servers hoard personal data. These companies could logically carry the blame for a massive attack. The best analogy is the financial crisis of 2008. There was nothing that the banks could do to gain political traction in the face of the catastrophe that they unleashed. When the Big One arrives, the tech companies will be vulnerable to the regulation that they have skillfully avoided. (Shamefully, there's no modern law governing the use of data.) Just as the financial crisis triggered the creation of Elizabeth Warren's Consumer Financial Protection Bureau—the rare launch of a new agency—the Big One has the potential for creating a sizable regulatory infrastructure.

What we need is a Data Protection Authority to protect privacy as the government protects the environment. Both the environment and privacy are goods that the market would destroy if left to its own devices. We let business degrade the environment within limits—and we should tolerate the same with privacy. The point isn't to prevent the collection or exploitation of data. What are needed, however, are constraints, about what can be collected and what can be exploited. Citizens should have the right to purge data that sits on servers. Rules should require companies to set default options so that citizens have to opt for surveillance, rather than passively accept the loss of privacy, a far more robust option than the incomprehensible take-it-or-leave-it terms of service agreements.

This is a matter of autonomy: The intimate details embedded in our data can be used to undermine us; data provides the basis for invisible discrimination; it is used to influence our choices, both our habits of consumption and our intellectual habits. Data provides an X-ray of the soul. Companies turn that photograph of the inner self into a commodity to be traded on a market, bought and sold without our knowledge.

It's a basic, intuitive right, worthy of enshrinement: Citizens, not the corporations that stealthily track them, should own their own data. The law should demand that these companies treat this data with the greatest care, because it doesn't belong to them. Possessing our data is a heavy responsibility that must come with ethical obligations. The American government has a special category for corporations that profit from goods that they don't truly own: We call them trustees. This is how the government treats radio and television broadcasters. Those companies make money from their use of the public airwaves, so the government requires that these broadcasters adhere to a raft of standards. At times, they were asked to broadcast civil defense warnings and public service announcements; they were asked to adhere to decency standards and were required to provide equal airtime to candidates of both political parties. The government, in the form of the Federal Communications Commission, supervises the broadcasters to guarantee that they don't shirk these obligations.

One of the most sacrosanct obligations of the data-driven firms is that they don't abuse their power to undermine democracy. The government shouldn't dictate the editorial policy of the platforms, but we should prevent our informational gatekeepers from suppressing criticism of themselves; we should insist that they provide equal access to a multiplicity of sources and viewpoints. I don't deny that this is a thicket of complex questions, which would require a legislative doorstop and many judicial rulings to untangle. This is not, however, a novel interpretation of the government's responsibilities. It's exactly what the Supreme Court has demanded of the state, even its most conservative justices. In 1994 Anthony Kennedy intoned, "Assuring the public has access to a multiplicity of information sources is a governmental purpose of the highest order."

IN A SHORT SPAN, we have moved very far from Justice Kennedy's view of government. It's the Europeans who have assumed the American mantle, though Americans prefer to mock them for that. And, it is true, the Europeans have occasionally struggled to articulate the basis for their hostility to the tech companies and their sundry efforts to block them. One reason for this difficulty is that they have instinctively veered far from their own political tradition, into strange terrain. Through its history, Europe has shown favor to cartels, giant corporations closely tied to the state. Until recently, the continent evinced little concern for the virtues of economic decentralization. It's not hard to ascribe self-serving motives to their sudden concern over the American tech giants— a desire to protect their own indigenous firms from American ones.

But before the United States damns Brussels's approach, it should stare in the mirror. Over the decades, the American state has done a first-rate job of limiting communications behemoths, allowing the oxygen for new technologies and new competitors. In the earliest days of the Republic, the postal service monopolized the flow of information. But with the advent of the telegraph, the government withstood the temptation to control the new medium, even though the postal service had ample opportunity to swallow it. The government allowed a period of rigorous private competition—which ended, as all such cycles do, with the rise of a monopoly: Western Union. Politicians, however, kept threatening to dismember Western Union, a threat that deterred Western Union from extending itself into telephony. AT&T emerged as the dominant firm in that new technology, but the government wouldn't let it extend into radio. When NBC achieved a grip over radio, the government insisted that it divide into two—NBC and ABC. The Nixon administration encouraged a challenge to the Big Three networks that controlled broadcasting, by promoting the emergence of cable. It's a noble, though sometimes imperfect, history of activism that has extended into our own era. The Clinton administration's case against Microsoft was quietly killed by the Bush administration in the aftermath of September 11, but the case put a scare into the software giant, which deterred it from repeating bad patterns of behavior. Instead of using its strength to strangle Google in its cradle, which was well within its power, it watched the upstart from a careful distance for fear of getting slapped by the government.

A Data Protection Authority would be the heir to this tradition. Unlike the Federal Trade Commission, which evaluates mergers to preserve low prices and economic efficiency, the authority would review them to protect privacy and the free flow of information. It would constrain monopolies as they attempt to carry their power into the next era, creating the opening through which challengers can ultimately emerge. The old Brandeisan view of antitrust needs to be hauled off the shelf—and though it might be a few moments premature, we shouldn't limit our policy imagination. The health of our democracy demands that we consider treating Facebook, Google, and Amazon with the same firm hand that led government to wage war on AT&T, IBM, and Microsoft—even dismembering them into smaller companies if circumstances (and the law) demand a forceful response. While it has been several generations since we wielded antitrust laws with such vigor, we should remember that these cases created the conditions that nurtured the invention of an open, gloriously innovative Internet in the first place.

Nearly thirty years after the fall of the Berlin Wall, after a terrible recession, and decades of growing inequality, regulation hasn't regained its reputation. In some ways, its stature has receded even further. Large swaths of the left now share the right's distaste for the regulatory state, a broad sense of indignation over corporations capturing the apparatus of the state. Instead of defending the people against big business, government becomes its servant.

But the long history of regulation also shows that the project is not nearly as futile as its critics claim. When government tries to remodel the economy for the sake of efficiency, it has amassed a mixed record. When government uses its power to achieve clear moral ends, it has a strong record. There are notable failures, for sure. But our automobiles are safer, our environment is cleaner, our food doesn't poison us, our financial system is fairer and less prone to catastrophic collapse, even though those protective provisions have imposed meaningful costs on the private sector. In the libertarian fervor that followed the fall of the Berlin Wall, we lost sight of this moral vision. The Internet is amazing, but we shouldn't treat it as if it exists outside history or is exempt from our moral structures, especially when the stakes are nothing less than the fate of individuality and the fitness of democracy.

Ten

THE ORGANIC MIND

WE KNOW FROM THE RECENT past that Silicon Valley is not destiny. It's possible to turn away from its monopolies. There's an example to illuminate the path—a precedent exists of consumers rejecting the primacy of convenience and low prices, where they have rebelled against homogenization. They have subsidized artisanal practices, which had been deemed doomed. The optimistic prospects for escaping the pull of Facebook, Google, and Amazon come in the form of yogurt, granola, and mâche.

A nontrivial percentage of the populace now stridently cares about what it puts in its mouth, which suggests it can be persuaded to apply the same care to what it ingests through the brain. Caring about the morality and quality of food has become a symbol of social status, which raises the question, why can't concern for books, essays, and journalism acquire the same cachet?

Back when Stewart Brand was editing the *Whole Earth Catalog*—peddling the artifacts of an alternative lifestyle to all the hippies who had retreated to the communes—he touted the promise of organic food. Food was as essential to the counterculture as drugs because the hippies were rebelling against a culture that placed food on a pedestal. During the Depression, Americans slipped into their beds feeling hungry. After the war, poverty began to dissipate. It was a world of genuine abundance, new suburbs with new supermarkets featuring a panoply of newly invented items. Food shouted its magical properties—Wonder Bread, Spam ("the miracle meat"), instant breakfast, Minute Rice. Advertisements touted new foods, like Tang, as space age achievements. What made these products so incredible was that they seemed to solve the essential problem of modernity, the crunch of time. At least that was the anxious-making pitch of television commercials, which warned there were no longer enough hours to cook. The freezer case would claw back the day.

It wasn't hard to see through this marketing hokum, and the counterculture did so with sneering disdain. "A fresh-frozen life in some prepackaged suburb," the intellectuals of the movement snapped. Butterball, Twinkies, and Jell-O perfectly symbolized everything amiss with postwar America. They were tasteless, conformist, and stamped with the imprint of corporate capitalism. Theodore Roszak wrote about the technocratic evils of Wonder Bread: "Not only do they provide bread aplenty, but the bread is as soft as floss; it takes no effort to chew, and yet it is vitamin-enriched." If you wanted to pick an object worthy of rebellion, an avatar of alienation, food wasn't a bad place to begin.

The hippies shoved all the store-bought crap from the plate and replaced it with a vision of goodness. Communes, with their back-to-the-land faith in self-sufficiency, cultivated gardens and raised livestock. Bohemian neighborhoods across the country opened nonprofit cooperatives with aisles of ethically produced food. Vegetarianism—once the relatively esoteric practice of Seventh-Day Adventists, Hindus, and assorted freethinkers—found a large following among the Woodstock set. An entirely new diet emerged, including such novel items as tofu and yogurt. The cultural critic Warren Belasco has written brilliantly about the semiotics of hippie cuisine. "White vs. brown was a central contrast. . . . Whiteness meant Wonder Bread, White Tower, Cool Whip, Minute Rice, instant mashed potatoes, peeled apples, White Tornadoes, white coats, white collar, whitewash, White House, white racism. Brown meant whole wheat bread, unhulled rice, turbinado sugar, wildflower honey, unsulfured molasses, soy sauce, peasant yams, 'black is beautiful.'"

The counterculture combined austere politics with hedonism, ethical righteousness, and corporeal pleasure. Food was in many ways the apotheosis of the movement. In the shadow of all that radicalism, the so-called Gourmet Ghetto flourished in Berkeley. Alice Waters transferred to the University of California just in time to witness the green shoots of activism there. The school's Free Speech Movement, with its charismatic leaders and utopian politics, transfixed her. Waters began to host salons, where she cooked for the likes of Huey Newton and Abbie Hoffman. Waters tied her cuisine to the Bay Area zeitgeist. Her ideal was the French food she tasted as an exchange student—food that wasn't frozen or canned, but intimately connected to the farm, forest, and sea. Through food, it was possible to achieve the holism that Stewart Brand touted, to see our interplanetary connection. ("Eating is a political act," Waters proclaimed.) In 1971, Waters opened Chez Panisse, arguably the most influential restaurant in American history. Through tarragon and escarole, Waters attempted to inject countercultural values into the mainstream.

It's an oft-told tale, how mainstream American society effortlessly absorbed the ethos of the counterculture. All that rebellious spirit was domesticated and turned into Madison Avenue slogans. Capitalism came to extol the virtues of rebellion and nonconformity. *Dare to be different*, the car commercial taunted. This is the story of food, of how a company like Celestial Seasonings went from a bunch of hippies selling herbal products to a company that does $100 million in annual sales; or how two Jewish transplants to Vermont, with a jones for the Grateful Dead, created an ice cream brand found in every 7-Eleven and Walmart; or how even McDonald's now sells salads full of once-exotic greens.

This merits cynicism, but also praise and awe. The journalist David Kamp has written that the transformation of the American diet might well be the counterculture's greatest and most lasting triumph. Wonder Bread America seemed an irreversible way of life. Although it hasn't been reversed, it has been dented. The ideal of farm-to-table cuisine—food that is minimally processed and grown locally—has fixed itself in the upper middle class. From there, it has started to spread to society at large, through the exhortations of Michelle Obama and the instruction of celebrity chefs.

Let's not mistake the food movement for a Marxist one. There's more than a hint of conspicuous consumption in the fetishization of heirloom tomatoes and the obeisance paid to slabs of grass-fed dry-aged beef. The rich have always used food to set themselves apart from the rest of us. Once hippies became yuppies, it was unavoidable that they would spend their disposable income on cuisine, which is what helped propel the rise of

Williams-Sonoma, the debut of the Food Network, and the whole era of gastropornography.

Still, in the farmers' markets and the Whole Foods, there remains something radical—a turn away from the cheap, mass-produced, and heavily marketed. Why have American consumers taken this unexpected turn? Okay, the food is often better, but sometimes it's indistinguishable in taste from the stuff that can be bought at Safeway. What they're really purchasing is the sensation of virtue and rectitude. Michael Pollan has written:

> Though seldom articulated as such, the attempt to redefine, or escape, the traditional role of consumer has become an important aspiration of the food movement. In various ways it seeks to put the relationship between consumers and producers on a new, more neighborly footing, enriching the kinds of information exchanged in the transaction, and encouraging us to regard our food dollars as "votes" for a different kind of agriculture and, by implication, economy. The modern marketplace would have us decide what to buy strictly on the basis of price and self-interest; the food movement implicitly proposes that we enlarge our understanding of both those terms, suggesting that not just "good value" but ethical and political values should inform our buying decisions, and that we'll get more satisfaction from our eating when they do.

These are aspirations worthy of transposition.

THERE ARE SIMILARITIES between the new corporate concentration in culture and the old corporate concentration in food. But we shouldn't simply cast blame on capitalist villainy. Just as the American consumer ushered in the age of the Twinkie, the American consumer is complicit in the degradation of the culture. Over the last two decades, readers have come to regard words as disposable goods. They pay shamefully little, if anything, for much of the writing they consume. That's a depressing truth, but it also contains the possibility for redemption: If readers helped create the conditions for monopolistic dominance, they also have the ability to reverse it.

Everything hinges on undoing the devil's bargain of advertising. Media has always subsisted on it. For most of their history, media lived off two streams of revenue. Readers paid for newspapers and magazines, either in the form of subscriptions or as copies bought at the newsstand. Subscriptions rarely covered the cost of printing and delivery, but that didn't matter. A publication's circulation file was evidence of a committed, captive audience—and the attention of that audience could be sold for a handsome profit to advertisers.

Because circulation was never a profitable business, the Internet hardly required a large leap of imagination. Instead of selling journalism to readers at a loss, media would give it away for nothing. Media executives bet everything on a fantasy: Publishing free articles on the Internet would enable newspapers and magazines to increase their readership manifold; advertising riches would follow the audience growth. It was a scenario that entranced nearly the entire industry, except the few brave contrarians with the steel to draw paywalls over their sites.

It might have worked, were it not for Google and Facebook. Newspapers and magazines assumed that the Web would be like a giant newsstand—and readers would remain attached to the sterling reputations of their titles, their distinctive sensibility, and brand-name writers. The new megaportals changed all that. They became the entry point for the Internet—and when readers entered, they hardly paid attention to the names attached to the journalism they read.

With their enormous scale, Facebook and Google could undercut media, selling ad space for phenomenally little because they had nearly infinite windows of display. Since they specialized in collecting data on their users, they could guarantee advertisers a precisely micro-targeted audience. By deflating the cost of advertising, Facebook and Google overthrew the entire go-with-your-gut expense-account regime that had dominated advertising for nearly a century. Indeed, you could buy their ads online—on Google the process is an automated auction—without having to deal with brokers and commissions. Textbook economics could have predicted the consequence of this deflation: As the media critic Michael Wolff has written, "To overcome falling ad prices you had to redouble audience growth."

Advertising has become an unwinnable battle. Facebook and Google will always beat media. Between 2006 and 2017, advertiser spending on newspapers dropped by nearly 75 percent, with most of that money redirected to Facebook and Google. Money shifted because the tech monopolists simply do a much better job of steadily holding the attention of audiences. Readers are committed to those platforms, returning to them all day long. Grabbing the attention of readers has become a very difficult project for media, often requiring trickery. Media increasingly rely on "drive-by traffic." Readers on Facebook and Google are conned into clicking on a piece, based on a carefully engineered headline, a provocative photo, or trendy subject matter. The *New York*

Times media reporter John Herrman mocked this mind-set: "Websites plausibly marketed these people as members of *their* audiences, rather than temporarily diverted members of a platform's audience. Wherever they came from, they were counted in the Chartbeat. They saw at least 50 percent of at least one ad for at least one second, and so they existed."

What's worse, victory in the traffic wars is slippery. Just as soon as a media outlet achieves its ambitious goals, advertisers deem those goals inadequate. Wolff has noted that advertisers keep shifting the targets ever higher. In 2010, a site needed about ten million unique visitors per month to score a meaningful buy. By 2014, that number rose to fifty million "uniques." There's no plausible strategy for growing at that clip, especially not a strategy that preserves editorial identity and integrity.

You know who foresaw the terrible tyranny of Internet advertising? Larry Page and Sergey Brin. They resisted turning Google into an advertising engine, at least at first. While they were still students at Stanford, they wrote a paper arguing, "We expect that advertising-funded search engines will be inherently biased toward the advertisers and away from the needs of consumers." It was such a worrying concern that they even doubted whether a trustworthy search engine could ever thrive in the marketplace. "We believe the issue of advertising causes enough mixed incentives that it is crucial to have a competitive search engine that is transparent and in the academic realm." They discarded their own wisdom long ago.

While media chase a fake audience, they consciously neglect their devoted readers. Subscribers to print editions are considered vestiges of a bygone era, even though they remain reliable sources of revenue. You might never know it from the digital rush, but circulation departments are efficient streams of revenue for many media companies. Still, it is often assumed that these readers will eventually die—and younger readers are habituated to never pay—so there is no point in growing their lot.

That assumption requires reversing. The time has arrived to liberate media from their reliance on advertising. Media need to scale back their ambitions, to return to their niches, to reclaim the loyalty of core audiences—a move that will yield superior editorial and sustainable businesses, even if such retrenchment would crush owners' (mostly delusional) fantasies of getting gobbled by conglomerates or launching IPOs. To rescue themselves, media will need to charge readers, and readers will need to pay.

IN 1946, George Orwell wrote a charming essay on a closely related subject, called "Books v. Cigarettes." The piece begins with Orwell, who had worked in a used-book shop, taking inventory of his own library. Orwell wasn't a quant. This is his only essay to include charts and tables. To be sure, the calculations weren't the most challenging. Orwell found that he had spent twenty-five pounds annually on books. In the grand scheme of his expenses, this was a trifle. "The cost of reading, even if you buy books instead of borrowing them and take in a fairly large number of periodicals, does not amount to more than the combined cost of smoking and drinking."

His point was that reading is one of the cheaper forms of recreation, yet it was widely considered an expensive hobby beyond the reach of the workingman. This was an assumption that the workingman internalized. The average British citizen spent one pound or less on books each year, which depressed Orwell to no end. He concluded his essay with this bit of sourness: "It is not a proud record for a country which is nearly 100 per cent literate and where the ordinary man spends more on cigarettes than an Indian peasant has for his whole livelihood. And if our book consumption remains as low as it has been, at least let us admit that it is because reading is a less exciting pastime than going to the dogs, the pictures or the pub, and not because books, whether bought or borrowed, are too expensive."

Of course, Orwell's subject was books. If we were to update his arguments, his primary concern would be journalism. Books, indeed, offer a measure of optimism. The American public paid good money to buy 652,673,000 hardcover books in 2015. So let's stop rationalizing the inane economics of magazines and newspapers. It's silly to assert that information wants to be free. That was a piece of nineties pablum that has survived far too long. Consumers have no inherent problem paying for words, so long as publishers place a price tag on them.

Orwell tried to provoke the public to spend on words by nagging his readers with wit, charm, and shame. He would surely deem his efforts a failure. But he wasn't wrong. The culture industry can indeed persuade consumers to spend on worthy texts. At the same time he was mulling these questions, a man on the other side of the Atlantic was showing how it could be done.

SIGMUND FREUD'S NEPHEW EDWARD BERNAYS arrived in New York as an infant. Far from Vienna, he still managed to become versed in his uncle's theories. As an adult, he found a novel application for them. Bernays took the theory of the subconscious and used it to create the profession of public relations. Early in his career, Bernays devised slogans for the Wilson administration to help float public support for World War I. After the peace, he took his techniques and turned them into a manifesto, as well as a business. He wrote the tract *Propaganda*, one of the most influential handbooks of the twentieth century. Bernays's devotees included Joseph Goebbels. (To be fair, Bernays declined to work for Hitler and Franco, both of whom solicited his services.) His firm concocted slogans and advertising campaigns for the biggest corporations in America. Bernays convinced Americans that bacon and eggs are the quintessential wholesome breakfast foods. He used subliminal images of vaginas and venereal diseases to help promote disposable Dixie Cups as the only sanitary method of drinking. "Propaganda," he wrote chillingly, "makes it possible for minority ideas to become effective more quickly."

In the 1930s, the New York book publishers were filled with existential dread. The stock market crash and ensuing Depression wounded their business. They were bereft of ideas that might stimulate revival. In their desperation, Simon & Schuster, Harcourt Brace, and others turned to Bernays for salvation. Bernays developed a thoroughgoing critique of book publishing, which he accused of underpricing its product. But he also came up with an ingenious formula for transforming the industry: bookshelves. "Where there are bookshelves, there will be books," he confidently asserted.

Bookshelves were alien to most American homes, a luxury reserved for Jay Gatsby and his kind. Bernays methodically went about introducing bookshelves to the middle class. He persuaded architects to include them in their plans and encouraged stories in magazines (*House Beautiful, American Home, Woman's Home Companion*) that celebrated built-in shelving. The shelves were obviously an adornment, but also more than that. The presence of books in the household was implicitly meant to signify social advancement—books were hallmarks of the ascendant professional class, whose jobs demanded intellectual skills; they were consumer goods that indicated purchasing power. The cultural historian Ted Striphas has written that the shelving fad of the interwar years represented "the allure of propriety and abundance, which could be realized not only through the consumption, but, equally important, through the accumulation and display of printed books."

The proliferation of bookshelves was hailed for injecting new life into publishing. An article in *Publishers Weekly* proclaimed, "We are profiting at the moment from the need for books in individual homes built during the past few years. . . . Now is the time to get behind it and keep going!" This phenomenon was a classic example of what the midcentury sociologist Erving Goffman described in his book *The Presentation of Self in Everyday Life*. He understood that we unfurl ourselves as if we are actors in a play. We choose props and sets to make our character more convincing. For the growing middle class, anxious about its place in the world, books created an impression of well-deserved elevation to the higher ranks of society.

The *New Yorker* serves as this sort of prop, read on the subway, displayed on the coffee table. Readers gaudily unfurl the magazine as a totem of their cosmopolitanism and literary bent. The *New Yorker* publishes its share of refined clickbait and self-help pieces (in the guise of social science). Still, the magazine has largely managed to wean itself of its dependence on advertising, shifting toward a financial reliance on its readers. (Even as the

New Yorker profited from advertising, it approached that income warily. (During his long reign as the magazine's editor, the famously prudish William Shawn frequently turned away advertising that he considered distasteful, especially lingerie ads.) The *New Yorker* has guarded the value of its prime property, its print magazine, by resisting the impulse to give away all of its pieces for free on the Internet.

Of course, the *New Yorker* occupies a unique place in the culture, always has. But it is possible to build cultural cachet from scratch. Strangely, it's the tech companies that have best pulled off that trick. Ads for the iPad show it as a method for reading the *New York Times* and the *New Yorker*, a way to pursue hobbies like astronomy and fine photography. Amazon's marketing features travelers sitting in cosmopolitan locales, Kindle in hand. They have billed themselves as both status symbols and the devices that will bring cultivation.

Here's where the food movement provides an object lesson. The culture industries need to present themselves as the organic alternative, a symbol of social status and aspiration. Media must denounce their most recent phase, to lead a rebellion against the processed, ephemeral, speed-based writing encouraged by the tech companies. Subscriptions are the route away from the aisles of clickbait. (The *New York Times* successfully marketed itself as a bulwark of democracy in the wake of Donald Trump's election, acquiring 130,000 subscribers in the immediate aftermath of that debacle, implicitly contrasting itself with Facebook's morass of conspiracy and falsehood.) Sure, it will always be possible to get lots of information online for nothing. But if enlightenment and virtue aren't free and easy, that's a reasonable price to pay.

AGRICULTURE AND CULTURE come from the Latin *colere*. The great critic Raymond Williams excavated the fossilized forerunner. "*Colere* had a range of meanings: inhabit, cultivate, protect, honour with worship," he wrote. When the Latin passed into English, it referred specifically to husbandry. Culture meant tending to the natural growth of crops and animals.

On the eve of the Enlightenment, the term became a metaphor for humans, who required tending, too. Most specifically, it was the mind that required attention, protection, and cultivation. Thomas More: "to the culture and profit of their minds"; Francis Bacon: "the culture and manurance of minds." "Culture" is a word that never settles into a stable meaning. Rather, we apply it promiscuously and infuse it with our own biases. Williams called culture "one of the two or three most complicated words in the English language."

Through the word's long, wending history, it retains traces of *colere*. Our faith in culture is diminishing, replaced by our mania for data, but we still worship at its shrines. We still believe that art, books, music, and film have the power to cultivate the self. This is the very thing that obsessed Louis Brandeis, his fixation on "developing the faculties."

We know this is a noble sentiment, but also a tinged one. To describe oneself as "cultured" is an assertion of superiority. The sociologist Pierre Bourdieu made a career of pointing this out, if a bit too emphatically. Bourdieu, the son of a peasant, grew up speaking a moribund dialect of French. He soared through the French meritocracy to the most rarefied heights of the intelligentsia. Once admitted to the club, he railed against it. Bourdieu argued that a dominant class enforces rules about what is and is not acceptable. It defines good art, good food, good books—and creates an exclusionary vocabulary for describing them. "Taste classifies, and it classifies the classifier," he famously wrote.

The world Bourdieu described was very French, a bit hard for an American to appreciate. Overt snobbery has largely foundered on the shoals of hamburger and apple pie. Another Frenchman, Alexis de Tocqueville, understood this. The nature of American society was to eschew elitism. In Tocqueville's account, elites interacted with workingmen as equals, even if their bank accounts told a different story (and even if our faith in equality bred rampant mediocrity). Cultural elites have made it their business to elevate the masses—an ethos that culminated in the glorious rise of the middlebrow culture of midcentury America. In those *anni mirabiles*, Henry Luce's publications hired serious writers (James Agee, Dwight Macdonald, John Hersey, Daniel Bell) and put serious intellectuals (Walter Lippmann, Reinhold Niebuhr, T. S. Eliot) on its covers, which were designed by serious artists (Fernand Léger, Diego Rivera, Rockwell Kent). NBC hired Arturo Toscanini to conduct its orchestra; Leonard Bernstein hosted a prime-time show on CBS to teach appreciation of symphonic music. The Book of the Month Club and the Readers' Subscription delivered literature to American homes on a regular basis.

A sense of noblesse oblige permeated these efforts—and a sense of status anxiety made the American public receptive to them. Thanks to the GI Bill, millions of Americans attended college, often the first in their families to make the trek beyond high school. The prosperity of the postwar years swelled the middle class. To validate their arrival in a higher social station, Americans swaddled themselves in higher culture. They filled the shelves that Bernays inspired with encyclopedias, leather-bound editions of classics, and hardcover novels. Art house cinema proliferated, because there was a meaningful market for Godard and Antonioni. Midsized cities sprouted symphony orchestras.

Not everything that flourished in this era was worthy of praise. "Middlebrow" became a term of derision for good reason. There was tension in the vision of culture. The elites that ran media and publishing, record labels and movie studios believed they were great patrons. But, of course, they were running commercial institutions. At their worst, they peddled mass-market novels posing as great art. At their best, they nurtured ambitious art and challenging ideas and sold them to society.

Our greatest companies in publishing and journalism have mythologized their mission; many are still varnishing themselves in a patina of nobility. This high-mindedness isn't hard to strip away. Those companies may pose as guardians of intellectual seriousness, but they also exist to turn a profit. They aren't latter-day Medicis, even if that's the sense of self that helps them through the day. The health of our culture, however, depends on the persistence of that mythology. It's the myth that ties these companies to *colere*, the old root of culture, a faith that they must cultivate minds. Without this myth, culture is just another market-pleasing commodity.

That myth is still standing, but only just. We're on the cusp of an age of algorithmically derived art and ideas. Machines are increasingly suggesting the most popular topics for human inquiry, and humans are increasingly obeying. Instead of experimentation and novelty, data is leading the way, propelling us toward formula. The myth of cultivation gives way to crass manipulation.

One common reaction to this change is resignation—fatalism in the face of technology's inevitable march and the shifting habits of rising generations. Criticizing change can feel like an act of fist-shaking grumpiness and standing athwart history. Better to be mature, the thinking goes. Better to accede and make the most of circumstances, to steadily navigate the roiling. But writers and editors know, deep down, that the compromises come at too great a price; some readers have a sense that superior alternatives exist. There are moments when we all seem to agree on this point. The election of Donald Trump came with the shock of collective recognition that our media culture has decayed—and a sense that we need more committed protectors of truth than the feckless gatekeepers at Facebook and Google. Grasping the problem is not enough. We need to permit our analysis of the problem to guide us to sweeping solutions before we irreversibly change our most important institutions and values.

Eleven

THE PAPER REBELLION

THERE IS A PIECE of technology hailed as inevitable, almost universally assumed to present consumers with an irresistible choice. It has fallen short of expectations—and in that gap between the hype and reality, we can see the public unconsciously gravitating toward a profound critique, the stirrings of a backlash.

When Jeff Bezos unveiled the first Kindle in 2007, I ordered it straightaway. As a lifelong fetishist of the book, this didn't quite feel right. But I withstood a surge of guilt about my small role in the metamorphosis of reading. In truth, the device was the invention of my dreams. The bookstore and the book, two of my favorite things, had merged into one piece of hardware. There was the promise that every volume in existence could be downloaded to the hand in less time than it took to yawn.

The device itself was wonky. It came with a keyboard that barely worked and an inelegant joystick that tested manual dexterity. Pages flipped at the wrong moment. The Kindle, however, was magic. I went on a spending spree—and unlike trips to the bookstore, the binges didn't culminate in messy piles and never filled me with guilt about all the unread volumes staring at my desk. For a year, the Kindle traveled in the outside pocket of my tote and slept on my side table. Its off-white shell acquired a blackish tint from the attention of my grubby paws.

On the Amazon site, it's possible to retrieve an inventory of the devices that one has registered to access Kindle editions, a personal history of hardware. Over time, I have owned three Kindles, three iPads, and six iPhones, the makings of a minor environmental catastrophe. To be clear, I keep the discarded gizmos in a box in the basement that will someday find its way to an appropriate recycling facility, maybe.

But if technology blinds us with its magic, the magic can wear off. By the time my third Kindle rolled in, I found myself returning to paper. My reversion wasn't self-conscious. It happened slowly. I never really stopped collecting physical books. Because I worked for a magazine, review copies would arrive in the office with the postman. And there were old books that I couldn't find on the Kindle, which I ordered from used-book sellers. The paper editions began to beckon. I didn't think much about my transition back to paper. It just magnetically occurred.

I have no principled or scientific objections to screens. The Internet is my home for most of the day. Twitter captures a huge share of my attention. I'm grateful for the rush of information, the microscopic way it is possible to follow politics and soccer and poetry and journalistic gossip. It's strange, though, to look back and recall a day's worth of reading. Of course, I could probably pose the question to my computer and find a precise record. But if I sit at my desk and try to list all the tweets and articles and posts that have crossed my transom, there are very few that I actually remember. Reading on the Web is a frantic activity, compressed, haphazard, not always absorbed.

Apologists for the Internet are very clear on the point. The Internet is a very different medium, which inspires its own rhythms and intellectual biases. Where paper is fixed—words on a page can't be changed; books have beginnings and endings—the Internet is fluid. As Kevin Kelly has written, the digital world proves that "good things don't have to be static, unchanging." The Internet is an unending conversation; every argument is rebutted, shared, revised, and extended. It is a real-time extension of happenings in the world, exhilarating and exhausting.

I suppose my abandonment of the Kindle is a response to this exhaustion. It's not that the Kindle is a terrible device. In fact, it's downright placid compared to the horns and jackhammers blaring on social media. But after so many hours on the Web, I crave escaping the screen, retreating to paper.

If I were to justify this choice, I would argue that the Kindle doesn't fully provide respite from the Web. The Kindle may tamp down the noise, but it still doesn't provide a state of isolation. Amazon tracks every movement across its e-books. It uses the data it gleans from Kindles to predict the commercial efficacy of the books it sells. It tracks the passages that we underline—and shares those markings with our fellow readers. It remains a fortress of big tech, umbilically connected to an exclusive store. The Kindle is an effective simulation of a book, yet it's still a simulation.

It was predicted that e-books would overtake the paper book, that they would become the totality of publishing. In 2010, the founder of MIT Media Lab, Nicholas Negroponte, was precise about the hour that paper would perish. "It's happening in 5 years." Well, doomsday has come and gone. Paper books have held their ground, and e-book sales have failed to accumulate at their predicted pace. Actually, they have plummeted. In 2015, e-book revenue dropped by 11 percent, while brick-and-mortar bookstore revenue increased by nearly 2 percent. My turn away from the Kindle wasn't an idiosyncrasy, but part of a widespread tendency. My hunch is that a good portion of the reading public wants an escape from the intense flow of the Internet; they want silent reading, private contemplation—and there's a nagging sense that paper, and only paper, can induce such a state. The popular gravitation back to the page—not the metaphorical page, but the fibrous thing you can rub between your fingers—is a gravitation back to fundamental lessons from the history of reading.

I APOLOGIZE FOR THE following disclosure, which isn't intended to implant any insoluble images: My favorite place to read is the tub. A warm soak, the platonic state of mental openness and relaxation but for the possibility of water damage to the page. If the tub is occupied by another member of my brood, I will tolerate the bed. Obese pillows behind the back, a strong lamp spotlighting the text.

It's a banal disclosure, really. These are quite common locales for reading, perhaps the most common. Indeed, the entire history of the printed word points toward consuming books in such intimate settings, toward reading alone in our places of refuge. We choose to read in private to escape, but also because of the intellectual possibilities that this escape creates.

During the early Middle Ages, the book was quite literally a miracle. It was the means by which a priest conveyed the word of

God. Literacy was sparse. In Europe, maybe one in one hundred people could read. As the historian Steven Roger Fischer puts it, "to read" was to read aloud. Silent reading was a highly unusual practice. There are only a handful of recorded instances of it, worthy of note because they so shocked observers. Reading was perhaps the ultimate social activity. Storytellers read to the market, priests read to their congregations, lecturers read to university students, the literate read aloud to themselves. Medieval texts commonly asked audiences to "lend ears."

Despite the relative intellectual bleakness of the era, literacy slowly crept beyond a small elite. The growth of commerce created the glimmerings of a new merchant class, along with professional texts that catered to its needs. Texts—once imposing blocks of letters, with one word jammed into the next, no white spaces separating them—were tamed by new syntactical rules. There were increasingly breaks between words, punctuation even. Reading grew less strenuous, more accessible. It took several hundred years for the changes to fully register, for public reading to give way to silent reading.

It was one of the most profound transformations in human history. Reading ceased to be a passive, collective experience. It became active and private. Silent reading changed thinking; it brought the individual to the fore. The act of private reading—in beds, in libraries—provided the space for heretical thought. Fischer described the change:

> Active silent reading now prevailed, which demanded engagement. Hereby a reader became a doer, insofar as an author was now merely a guide who showed her or his silent and invisible audience a variety of paths. If early medieval listener-readers

had almost always heard one chorus of voices singing Christian litany in harmonized unison, "humanist" scholars of the late Middle Ages were silently reading an entire world of voices, each singing a different song and in many tongues. . . . After generations of weaning from the oral thrall, countless readers could at last admit like Thomas à Kempis in *The Imitation of Christ*: "I have sought for happiness everywhere, but I have found it nowhere except in a little corner with a little book."

There's a strong impulse in our culture to run away from these little corners. We're told that society's winners will be the thinkers who network, collaborate, create, and strategize in concert with others. Our kids are taught to study in groups, to execute projects as teams. Our workplaces have been stripped of walls so that the organization functions as a unit. The big tech companies also propel us to join the crowd—they provide us with the trending topics and their algorithms suggest that we read the same articles, tweets, and posts as the rest of the world.

There's no doubting the creative power of conversation, the intellectual potential of humbly learning from our peers, the necessity of groups working together to solve problems. Yet none of this should replace contemplation, moments of isolation, where the mind can follow its own course to its own conclusions.

We read in our little corners, our beds and tubs and dens, because we have a sense that these are the places where we can think best. I have spent my life searching for an alternative. I will read in the café and on the subway, making a diligent, wholehearted effort to focus the mind. But it never entirely works. My mind can't shake its awareness of the humans in the room.

When we read deeply and with full commitment, we enter an almost trancelike state that mutes the outside world. The distance between words on the page and the scampering abstractions in our head collapses. As with the first generations of silent readers, heretical thoughts come and go; we're stripped of intellectual inhibitions. That's why we habitually retreat with our book to private spaces, where we don't need to worry about social conventions, where the world can't possibly read over our shoulder. That's why we can't jettison paper, even though the tech companies have tried their hardest to bring that about.

If the tech companies hope to absorb the totality of human existence into their corporate fold, then reading on paper is one of the few slivers of life that they can't fully integrate. The tech companies will consider this an engineering challenge waiting to be solved. Everyone else should take regular refuge in the sanctuary of paper. It is our respite from the ever-encroaching system, a haven we should self-consciously occupy. Our model for resistance is the Czech novelist.

MILAN KUNDERA WAS THE DIRTIEST novelist of his era. He was the laureate of the orgy, the great stylist of bedroom humiliation, the literary explicator of transgressive copulation in its full diversity. To be sure, this obsession hardly distinguished him from other Czech authors of his time. Josef Škvorecký and Ivan Klíma also wrote lots of sex—rampant, promiscuous, graphic—into their tales. They penned masterworks of titillation, though that wasn't wholly the point. A totalitarian society attempts to obliterate private life, whereas the novelist seeks to inhabit it. Sex was an obsession because it seemingly provided an antidote to the omniscient state. It was a realm, a genuine human experience, uncontrolled by the state.

Surveillance on the Internet is far different from the monitoring of the totalitarian state. The Soviet Union and its family of nations watched citizens to breed paranoia, to enforce the dogmas of the party, and ultimately to preserve a small elite's undemocratic hold on power. We're watched on the Internet so that companies can more effectively sell us goods.

The fact that Internet surveillance isn't totalitarian, however, doesn't mean that it does us no harm. We're watched so that we can be manipulated. Some of this manipulation is welcome. We might revel in algorithmic recommendations of music, we're pleased to be shown an advertisement for sneakers, we need computer help sifting through the mass of information. But there's another way to describe the convenience of the machine: It is the surrender of free will—algorithms make choices for us. This isn't so terrible, because our submission to manipulation is largely willing. Yet we rightly have a sense that we're surrendering far more than we intend and that we're being manipulated far more than we know.

Our digital future may be as glorious as advertised, or it could be a dystopian hell. But as citizens and readers, there's good reason to throw sand in the machine. Only government policy can really dent the monopolies that increasingly control the world of ideas. But we can find moments when we willfully remove ourselves from the orbit of these companies and their ecosystems. It's not a matter of dropping out, but of giving ourselves moments to ourselves.

The Czech novelists searched for the seams in the state, where they might escape watchful eyes. Paper—in the form of books, magazines, and newspapers—is the seam that we can inhabit. It's the place beyond the monopolies, where we don't leave a data trail, where we are untracked. When we read words on paper, we're removed from the notifications, pings, and other urgencies summoning us away from our thoughts. The page permits us, for a time in our day, to decouple from the machine, to tend to our human core.

THE QUESTIONS AT THE HEART of this book are especially sticky for Americans. Over our history, we've considered ourselves the vanguard of twin revolutions, one scientific, the other political. We've posed as the world's great incubator of technology, its premier inventor—which perfectly expressed our national character, our experimental republic, with its frontiersmen venturing into the unknown. This revolution in engineering was, of course, intimately connected to the American Revolution. Both were products of the same Enlightenment. They carried the same faith in reason. Our great early technologists—Franklin, Jefferson—were profound exponents of political liberty. The United States loudly promoted the gospels of technology and individualism, evangelically spreading them over the globe. We innovated relentlessly in both—creating lightbulbs and the right to privacy, the assembly line and the protection of speech.

The twin revolutions abetted each other. They pushed forward together, with only fleeting moments of tension. For the most part, our liberty created an economy—dynamic, iconoclastic—that strongly incentivized the act of creation. And inventions furthered the cause of liberty, allowing for new means of personal expression, freedom of mobility, the fulfillment of self.

That's why the present moment feels so profoundly uncomfortable. Our faith in technology is no longer fully consistent with our belief in liberty. We're nearing the moment when we will have to damage one of our revolutions to save the other. Privacy can't survive the present trajectory of technology. Our ideas about the competitive marketplace are at risk. The proliferation of falsehood and conspiracy through social media, the dissipation of our common basis for fact, is creating conditions ripe for authoritarianism. Over time, the long merger of man and machine has worked out pretty well for man. But we're pulling into a new era, when that merger threatens the individual.

Human nature is malleable. It's not some fixed thing, but has a breaking point, a point at which our nature is no longer really human. We might decide to sail happily past that threshold, but we need to be honest about the costs. Right now, we're not steering our course. We're drifting without countervailing pressure from the political system, from media, or from the intelligentsia. We're drifting toward monopoly, conformism, their machines.

In this era of rapid automation, when the Internet connects to nearly everyone and everything, the thought of steering our own course can feel foolish and futile. "Our very mastery seems to escape our mastery," the philosopher Michel Serres has argued. "How can we dominate our domination?" It's a fretful question, but it also implies that humans have untapped reserves of agency. Technology companies aspire to pattern our lives and habits, yet the lives and habits remain ours. Perhaps as a society we will spring to our senses and impose the wise policies of state that protect the culture, democracy, and the individual from the corrosiveness of these corporations. In the meantime, we need to protect ourselves.

We have deluded ourselves into caring more deeply about convenience and efficiency than about the things that last. Compared to the sustaining nourishment of the contemplative life and the deep commitment to text, many of the promiscuous pleasures of the Web are vanishing. The contemplative life remains freely available to us through our choices—what we read and buy, how we commit to leisure and self-improvement, the passing over of empty temptation, our preservation of the quiet spaces, an intentional striving to become the masters of our mastery.

Acknowledgments

This a book about the world of ideas and about what happens when we no longer properly value that world. I hope that I will always remember to express my gratitude for the intellectual communities in which I have been so fortunately embedded.

Many of the core concepts for this book emerged from Leon Wieseltier's office, where I used to spend nearly every afternoon, discussing the issues of the moment and the timeless books on his shelves. For nearly two decades, he has been my friend, colleague, and teacher. The book improved immeasurably from close, generous readers. It especially benefited from the shrewd, careful guidance of Rachel Morris, a brilliant editor. I'm forever grateful to David Greenberg, Barry Lynn, Nicholas Lemann, Maurice Stucke, and Jacob Weisberg for their suggestions. I received first-rate research help from Hillary McClellen and Jessie Roberts. When I needed intellectual comradery, Anne-Marie Slaughter and Peter Bergen of the New America Foundation provided me just that. Along the way, I benefited from the continued guidance of my old *New Republic* colleagues and friends: Jonathan Chait, Isaac Chotiner, John B. Judis, Alec MacGillis, Chris Orr, Jeffrey Rosen, Michael Schaffer, Noam Scheiber, Judith Shulevitz, Amanda Silverman, Andrew Sullivan, Greg Veis, and Jason Zengerle. Thanks also to Susan Athey, Thomas Catan, Alan Davidson, Tom Freedman, Peter Fritsch, Jeffrey Goldberg, Jonathan Kanter, Jodi Kantor, Larry Kramer, Roger Noll, and Terry Winograd.

There's a reason that Ann Godoff is regarded as publishing's finest. She could see the trajectory of my argument far better than I initially glimpsed it; she paid close attention to detail, while remaining a visionary. She has also assembled a murders' row at Penguin Press: William Heyward, Casey Rasch, Scott Moyers, Elisabeth Calamari. Bea Hemming of Jonathan Cape, in the UK, was devoted to this project from the start, as was my friend and agent, Rafe Sagalyn.

My brothers helped lift me up many time along the way, and my parents somehow delicately balanced honest criticism and exuberant support. This book ends on an optimistic note, because I have Theo and Sadie, naturally born idealists and the best company. With all my heart, thanks to my wife, Abby. She has supplied me with the love, encouragement, and wisdom to make it all the way through the challenges of writing and life.

Notes

CHAPTER ONE: THE VALLEY IS WHOLE, THE WORLD IS ONE

12 **as an "Indian freak":** Tom Wolfe, *The Electric Kool-Aid Acid Test* (Farrar, Straus & Giroux, 1968), 2, 11.

12 **child of an advertising executive:** For biographical details about Brand, I leaned heavily on three excellent books: Fred Turner, *From Counterculture to Cyberculture* (University of Chicago Press, 2006); John Markoff, *What the Dormouse Said* (Viking Penguin, 2005); Walter Isaacson, *The Innovators* (Simon & Schuster, 2014).

13 **"cosmic consciousness":** Turner, 59.

13 **"tend to be extra-planetary":** Sherry L. Smith, *Hippies, Indians, and the Fight for Red Power* (Oxford University Press, 2012), 52.

13 **"a peyote meeting without peyote":** Charles Perry, *The Haight-Ashbury* (Random House, 1984), 19.

14 **messing around with acid:** Markoff, 61.

14 **he represented the "restrained, reflective wing":** Wolfe, 12.

15 **"scorned computers as the embodiment of centralized control":** Isaacson, 268.

15 **"operation of the machine becomes so odious":** Turner, 11.

16 **"Please do not fold, bend, spindle or mutilate me":** Turner, 2.

16 **"Defense Calculator":** Paul E. Ceruzzi, *A History of Modern Computing* (MIT Press, 2003), 34–35.

16 **"were not at odds with the Soviet political system":** Ceruzzi, 12.

17 **"Oh Wow! confabulation":** Theodore Roszak, *From Satori to Silicon Valley* (Don't Call It Frisco Press, 1986), 16–17.

18 **commune population swelled to 750,000:** Judson Jerome, *Families of Eden* (Seabury Press, 1974), 18.

18 **"a way to be of use to communes":** "From Counterculture to Cyberculture: The Legacy of the *Whole Earth Catalog*," Stanford University symposium, November 9, 2006.

18 **"one of the bibles of my generation":** Steve Jobs, Stanford University commencement address, June 12, 2005.

19 **"We are as gods":** *Whole Earth Catalog*, Fall 1968.

20 **"We can't put it together. It is together":** *The Last Whole Earth Catalog*, June 1971.

20 **"[The catalog] helped create the conditions":** Turner, 73.

21 **"he was the guy who was giving us the early warning system":** Katherine Fulton, "How Stewart Brand Learns," *Los Angeles Times*, October 30, 1994.

22 **"Those magnificent men with their flying machines":** Stewart Brand, "Spacewar: Fanatic Life and Symbolic Death Among the Computer Bums," *Rolling Stone*, December 7, 1972.

22 **"When computers become available to everybody":** Brand, "Spacewar."

22 **injected an important new phrase into the lexicon:** Stewart Brand, *II Cybernetic Frontiers* (Random House, 1974).

23 **"Ever since there were two organisms":** Turner, 121.

24 **"Today, after more than a century":** Marshall McLuhan, *Understanding Media* (McGraw-Hill, 1964), 3.

25 **"desert of classified data":** Eric McLuhan and Frank Zingrone, eds., *Essential McLuhan* (Basic Books, 1995), 92.

25 **"Today computers hold out the promise":** McLuhan, 80.

26 **"Life will be happier for the on-line individual":** Isaacson, 261.

26 **"Hope in life comes from the interconnections":** Tim Berners-Lee, *Weaving the Web* (HarperCollins, 1999), 209.

27 **"Money is not the greatest of motivators":** Linus Torvalds, *Just for Fun* (HarperCollins, 2001), 227.

29 **"Competition means strife":** Tim Wu, *The Master Switch* (Alfred A. Knopf, 2010), 8.

29 **"America's most famous financier":** Ron Chernow, *The House of Morgan* (Atlantic Monthly Press, 1990), 54.

30 **"We preach competition":** Peter Thiel, *Zero to One* (Crown Business, 2014), 35.

30 **"transcend the daily brute struggle":** Thiel, 32.

31 **"The big technology markets actually tend to be winner take all":** Alexia Tsotsis, "Marc Andreessen On The Future Of Enterprise," *TechCrunch*, January 27, 2013.

Chapter Two: The Google Theory of History

33 **at times, he struggled to breathe:** Larry Page, University of Michigan commencement address, May 2, 2009. My description of Carl Page relies heavily on my conversations with several of his colleagues from Michigan State, such as Hsu Wen Jing. The Page family requested that his closest friends decline interviews with reporters, so they spoke with me on the condition of anonymity.

34 **his dad brought home an Exidy Sorcerer:** Verne Kopytoff, "Larry Page's Connections," *San Francisco Chronicle*, December 31, 2000.

34 **"I think I was the first kid in my elementary school":** Larry Page interview, Academy of Achievement, October 28, 2000.

34 **convert Legos into an ink-jet printer:** David A. Vise and Mark Malseed, *The Google Story* (Delacorte, 2005), 24.

35 **build a computing outpost on a periphery of the digital world:** Vise and Malseed, 22.

35 **Grateful Dead concerts:** Vise and Malseed, 22.

36 **"In each case a central concept restructures understanding":** Sherry Turkle, *The Second Self* (Simon & Schuster, 1984), 247.

37 **his father had instructed him with religious intensity:** Ken Auletta, *Googled* (Penguin Press, 2009), 28, 32.

37 **Carl broke from his jovial form:** Larry Page, Google I/O 2013 Keynote, May 15, 2013.

38 **"it's AI complete":** Larry Page, "Envisioning the Future for Google: Always a Search Engine?" (lecture, Stanford University, Stanford, CA, May 1, 2002.)

38 **"directly attached to your brain":** Steven Levy, "All Eyes on Google," *Newsweek*, April 11, 2004.

38 **"a little version of Google":** Vise and Malseed, 281.

40 **Horrified by his discovery, the captain dragged Descartes's creation:** Stephen Gaukroger, *Descartes* (Oxford University Press, 1995), 1.

41 **"an extended, non-thinking thing":** Steven Nadler, *The Philosopher, the Priest, and the Painter* (Princeton University Press, 2013), 106.

41 **"prison of the body":** David F. Noble, *The Religion of Technology* (Alfred A. Knopf, 1997), 144.

41 **"I am a thinking thing":** Nadler, 107.

42 **"I shall now close my eyes":** Noble, 145.

42 **"He believed that his philosophical method":** Noble, 147.

43 **"The seclusion of a medieval monastery":** Isaacson, 41.

43 **"the gift for solitary thinking":** Stuart Hampshire, "Undecidables," *London Review of Books*, February 16, 1984.

43 **"One day ladies will take their computers for walks":** Andrew Hodges, *Alan Turing* (Vintage, 2012), 418.

44 **"We may hope that machines will eventually compete":** B. Jack Copeland, ed., *The Essential Turing* (Oxford University Press, 2004), 463.

45 **His parents, Viennese Jews, fled on the eve of the Anschluss:** Ray Kurzweil, Ask Ray blog, "My Trip to Brussels, Zurich, Warsaw, and Vienna," December 14, 2010.

45 **he made an appearance on Steve Allen's game show, *I've Got a Secret*:** Ray Kurzweil, "I've Got a Secret," 1965, https://www.youtube.com/watch?v=X4Neivqp2K4.

45 **"to invent things so that the blind could see":** Steve Rabinowitz quoted in *Transcendent Man*, directed by Barry Ptolemy, 2011.

46 "profoundly sad, lonely feeling that I really can't bear it": *Transcendent Man*.

47 **"strong AI and nanotechnology can create any product":** Ray Kurzweil, *The Singularity Is Near* (Viking Penguin, 2005), 299.

47 **"Each epoch of evolution has progressed more rapidly":** Kurzweil, *Singularity*, 40.

47 **"version 1.0 biological bodies":** Kurzweil, *Singularity*, 9.

48 **"We will be software, not hardware":** Ray Kurzweil, *The Age of Spiritual Machines* (Viking Penguin, 1999), 129.

48 **"What, after all, is the difference between a human":** Kurzweil, *Spiritual Machines*, 148.

48 **"Virtual sex will provide sensations that are more intense":** Kurzweil, *Spiritual Machines*, 147.

48 **"Anybody who is going to be resisting":** Peter Diamandis, quoted in *Transcendent Man*.

48 **"Our civilization will then expand outward":** Kurzweil, *Singularity*, 389.

49 **"Apocalyptic AI is the legitimate heir":** Robert M. Geraci, "Apocalyptic AI: Religion and the Promise of Artificial Intelligence," *Journal of the American Academy of Religion* 76, no. 1 (March 2008): 158–59.

49 **once said that he wanted to live to 102 so that he could laugh:** Wendy M. Grossman, "Artificial Intelligence Is Still the Future," *The Inquirer*, April 7, 2008.

49 **"the best person I know at predicting the future of artificial intelligence":** Kurzweil, *Singularity*, back cover.

49 **"represents a community of many of Silicon Valley's best and brightest":** John Markoff, *Machines of Loving Grace* (HarperCollins, 2015), 85.

50 **Google invests vast sums:** Alphabet Inc., Research & Development Expenses, 2015, Google Finance.

50 **"Google is not a conventional company":** Larry Page and Sergey Brin, "Letter from the Founders: 'An Owner's Manual' for Google's Shareholders," August 2004.

51 **The aphorism became widely known only:** Josh McHugh, "Google vs. Evil," *Wired*, January 2003.

51 **"We're at maybe 1%":** Greg Kumparak, "Larry Page Wants Earth to Have a Mad Scientist Island," *TechCrunch*, May 15, 2003.

52 **"This is the culmination of literally 50 years":** Robert D. Hof, "Deep Learning," *Technology Review*, www.technologyreview.com/s/513696/deep-learning.

52 **"The Google policy on a lot of things is to get right up to the creepy line":** Sara Jerome, "Schmidt: Google gets 'right up to the creepy line'," *The Hill*, October 1, 2010.

53 **Singularity University:** David Rowan, "On the Exponential Curve: Inside Singularity University," *Wired*, May 2013.

53 **Google has donated millions so that students can attend SU:** "Google Pledges $3 Million to Singularity University to Make Graduate Studies Program Free of Charge," *Singularity Hub*, January 28, 2015.

53 **"If I were a student, this is where I would like to be":** Exponential Advisory Board brochure, Singularity University.

53 **"One of the things I thought was amazing":** "*Time* Talks to CEO Larry Page About Its New Venture to Extend Human Life," *Time*, September 18, 2013.

54 **"There was a cloak-and-dagger element to the procedure":** Steven Levy, *In the Plex* (Simon & Schuster, 2011), 354.

54 **"If you don't have a reason to talk about it, why talk about it?":** Levy, *In the Plex*, 355.

54 **"Google's leadership doesn't care terribly much about precedent or law":** Levy, *In the Plex*, 353.

55 **"We are not scanning all those books to be read by people":** George Dyson, *Turing's Cathedral* (Pantheon, 2012), 312–13.

55 **"Being negative is not how we make progress":** Page, Google Keynote, May 15, 2013.

55 **"How exciting is it to come to work if the best you can do":** Steven Levy, "Google's Larry Page on Why Moon Shots Matter," *Wired*, January 17, 2013.

55 **how Google will someday employ more than one million people:** Levy, *Wired*, January 17, 2013.

Chapter Three: Mark Zuckerberg's War on Free Will

58 **But they were really small-minded paper-pushers:** Steven Levy, *Hackers* (O'Reilly Media, 2010), 29, 96.

58 **a box that enabled free long-distance calls:** Markoff, *Dormouse*, 272.

58 **In high school—using the *nom de hack* Zuck Fader:** Patrick Gillespie, "Was Mark Zuckerberg an AOL Add-on Developer?," patorjk.com, April 9, 2013.

58 **"One thing is certain," he wrote on a blog:** Ben Mezrich, *The Accidental Billionaires* (Anchor Books, 2009), 49.

59 **"We've got this whole ethos that we want to build a hacker culture":** Levy, *Hackers*, 475.

59 **"just this group of computer scientists who were trying to quickly prototype":** "Facebook CEO Mark Zuckerberg on stumbles: 'There's always a next move,'" *Today*, February 4, 2014.

60 **"Move Fast and Break Things":** "Mark Zuckerberg's Letter to Investors: 'The Hacker Way,'" *Wired*, February 1, 2012.

60 **"It was always very important for our brand":** David Kirkpatrick, *The Facebook Effect* (Simon & Schuster, 2010), 144.

60 **"radical transparency" or "ultimate transparency":** Kirkpatrick, 209.

61 **"The days of you having a different image for your work friends":** Kirkpatrick, 199.

61 **"To get people to this point where there's more openness":** Kirkpatrick, 200.

61 **"In a lot of ways Facebook is more like a government":** Kirkpatrick, 254.

62 **"Software is eating the world":** Marc Andreessen, "Why Software Is Eating the World," *Wall Street Journal*, August 20, 2011.

63 **"You have to make *words* less human":** Laura M. Holson, "Putting a Bolder Face on Google," *New York Times*, February 8, 2009.

63 **"You know I'm an engineer":** Ben Thompson, "Why Twitter Must Be Saved," Stratechery, November 8, 2016.

65 **"When one compares . . . one's own small talents with those of a Leibniz":** Matthew Stewart, *The Courtier and the Heretic* (W. W. Norton, 2006), 12.

66 **If ten can't be divided by six, and six can't be divided by ten:** Umberto Eco, *The Search for the Perfect Language* (Blackwell, 1995), 274.

66 **Sadly, whenever he tested the machine for an audience:** Stewart, 141.

67 **"Once this has been done, if ever further controversies should arise":** Eco, 281.

67 **He explained how automation of white-collar jobs:** James Gleick, *The Information* (Pantheon, 2011), 93.

67 **The essence of the algorithm is entirely uncomplicated:** John MacCormick, *Nine Algorithms That Changed the Future* (Princeton University Press, 2012), 3–4.

70 **"We can stop looking for models. We can analyze the data without hypotheses":** Chris Anderson, "The End of Theory: The Data Deluge Makes the Scientific Method Obsolete," *Wired*, June 23, 2008.

70 **Walmart's algorithms found that people desperately buy strawberry Pop-Tarts:** Constance L. Hays, "What Wal-Mart Knows About Customers' Habits," *New York Times*, November 14, 2004.

71 **Sweeney conducted a study that found that users with African American names:** Latanya Sweeney, "Discrimination in Online Ad Delivery," *Communications of the ACM* 56, no. 5 (May 2013): 44–54.

72 **Every product you use:** *Charlie Rose Show*, November 7, 2011.

72 **a "personalized newspaper":** Alexandra Chang, "Liveblog: Facebook Reveals a 'New Look for News Feed'," *Wired*, March 7, 2013.

73 **Many users—60 percent, according to the best research:** Motahhare Eslami, Aimee Rickman, Kristen Vaccaro, Amirhossein Aleyasen, Andy Vuong, Karrie Karahalios, Kevin Hamilton, and Christian Sandvig, "I always assumed that I wasn't really that close to [her]: Reasoning about Invisible Algorithms in News Feeds," *CHI'15 Proceedings of the 33rd Annual ACM Conference on Human Factors in Computing Systems*, April 2015, 153–62.

73 **"We have, perhaps for the first time ever, built machines we do not understand":** Jon Kleinberg and Sendhil Mullainathan, "We Built Them, But We Don't Understand Them," *Edge*, 2015.

75 **"a microscope that not only lets us examine social behavior":** Tom Simonite, "What Facebook Knows," *Technology Review*, June 13, 2012.

75 **Facebook sought to discover whether emotions are contagious:** Adam D. I. Kramer, Jamie E. Guillory, and Jeffrey T. Hancock, "Experimental evidence of massive-scale emotional contagion through social networks," *Proceedings of the National Academy of Sciences* 111, no. 24 (June 17, 2014): 8788–90.

75 **"Anyone on that team could run a test":** Reed Albergotti, "Facebook Experiments Had Few Limits; Data Science Lab Conducted Tests on Users With Little Oversight," *Wall Street Journal*, July 2, 2014.

75 **"It is possible that more of the .60% growth in turnout between 2006 and 2010":** Robert M. Bond, Christopher J. Fariss, Jason J. Jones, Adam D. I. Kramer, Cameron Marlow, Jaime E. Settle, and James H. Fowler, "A 61-Million-Person Experiment in Social Influence and Political Mobilization," *Nature* 489, no. 7415 (September 13, 2012): 295–98.

76 **Facebook can predict users' race, sexual orientation, relationship status, and drug use:** Michal Kosinski, David Stillwell, and Thore Graepel, "Private traits and attributes are predictable from digital records of human behavior," *Proceedings of the National Academy of Sciences* 110, no. 15 (April 9, 2013), 5802–5.

76 **"a fundamental mathematical law underlying human social relationships":** Michael Rundle, "Zuckerberg: telepathy is the future of Facebook," *Wired*, July 1, 2015.

76 **Some news wires use algorithms to write stories:** Joanna Plucinska, "How an Algorithm Helped the LAT Scoop Monday's Quake," *Columbia Journalism Review*, March 18, 2014.

CHAPTER FOUR: JEFF BEZOS DISRUPTS KNOWLEDGE

80 **"I'm grumpy when I'm forced to read a physical book":** "Jeff Bezos in Conversation with Steven Levy," *Wired* Business Conference, June 15, 2009.

80 **creating an "everything store":** Brad Stone, *The Everything Store* (Little, Brown and Company, 2013), 24.

83 **Adam Smith, it's fair to say, didn't anticipate Jeff Bezos:** My discussion of the economics of knowledge relies on David Warsh's excellent *Knowledge and the Wealth of Nations* (W.W. Norton, 2006).

84 **called "rivalry"—if I own a shovel, you can't own that shovel:** Paul M. Romer, "Endogenous Technological Change," *Journal of Political Economy* 98, no. 5 (October 1990): S71–102.

85 **"We can't stop copying on the Internet, because the Internet is a copying machine":** Cory Doctorow, *Information Doesn't Want to Be Free* (McSweeney's, 2014), 41.

86 **"The defining feature of the Internet is that it leaves resources free":** Lawrence Lessig, *The Future of Ideas* (Random House, 2001), 14.

87 **"Value is derived from plentitude":** Kevin Kelly, *New Rules for the New Economy* (Viking Penguin, 1998), 40.

87 **"atomic unit of consumption for news":** Astra Taylor, *The People's Platform* (Metropolitan Books, 2014), 204.

88 **Between 2006 and 2012, the world's information output grew tenfold:** Paul Mason, *Postcapitalism* (Farrar, Straus and Giroux, 2015), 125.

88 **"What information consumes is rather obvious":** Herbert A. Simon, "Designing Organizations for an Information-Rich World," in Martin Greenberger, ed., *Computers, Communications, and the Public Interest* (Johns Hopkins University Press, 1971), 40.

89 **"Searching and filtering are all that stand between this world and the Library of Babel":** Gleick, 410.

89 **But he initially refused to build the iPod so that it would block unlicensed content:** Chris Ruen, *Freeloading* (OR Books, 2012), 7.

90 **"Google has as much interest in free online media as General Motors does in cheap gasoline":** Robert Levine, *Free Ride* (Doubleday, 2011), 9.

90 **"pressure premium content providers to change their model":** Scott Cleland, "Grand Theft Auto-mated," *Forbes,* November 30, 2011.

92 **"Our goal is to give every person a voice":** Mark Zuckerberg, Facebook post, November 12, 2016.

CHAPTER FIVE: KEEPERS OF THE BIG GATE IN THE SKY

95 **"Seven years of declining revenues will give you new ideas":** Staci D. Kramer, "Don Graham on the Sale of The Washington Post, Jeff Bezos, and the Pace of Newsroom Innovation," *NiemanLab,* August 6, 2013.

96 **White had struck up a correspondence with an editor:** David Manning White, "The 'Gate Keeper': A Case Study in the Selection of News," *Journalism Quarterly* 27 (December 1950): 383–90.

97 **"So long as there is interposed between the ordinary citizen and the facts":** Walter Lippmann, *Liberty and the News* (Harcourt, Brace and Howe, 1920), 7.

98 **"The newspaper's duty is to its readers and to the public at large":** John B. Judis, *The Paradox of American Democracy* (Pantheon, 2000), 23.

98 **"News was to be separate from editorial judgment":** Judis, *Paradox,* 22.

99 **"Katie Graham's gonna get her tit caught in a big fat wringer":** Katharine Graham, *Personal History* (Alfred A. Knopf, 1997), 465.

99 **"hated for the *Post* or its writers to look as though they were":** David Halberstam, *The Powers That Be* (Knopf, 1975), 188.

101 **"Even well-meaning gatekeepers slow innovation":** Jeff Bezos, Letter to Amazon shareholders, 2011.

101 **"I see the elimination of gatekeepers everywhere":** Thomas L. Friedman, "Do You Want the Good News First?," *New York Times,* May 19, 2012.

101 **"The most radical and transformative of inventions are often those that empower":** Bezos, Letter, 2011.

102 **"Take a look at the Kindle bestseller list, and compare it":** Bezos, Letter to shareholders, 2011.

102 **"Our touchstone will be readers":** Jeff Bezos, "Jeff Bezos on *Post* Purchase," *Washington Post*, August 5, 2013.

105 **Amazon, on the other hand, considers the profession to be filled with "antediluvian losers":** George Packer, "Cheap Words," *New Yorker*, February 17, 2014.

105 **"should approach these small publishers the way a cheetah would pursue a sickly gazelle":** Stone, *Everything*, 243.

106 **"No technology, not even one as elegant as the book, lasts forever":** Daniel Lyons, "Why Bezos Was Surprised by the Kindle's Success," *Newsweek*, December 20, 2009.

107 **"By the early twenty-first century, literally 99.9 percent of contemporary daily papers":** Ben H. Bagdikian, *The New Media Monopoly* (Beacon Press, 2004), 121.

107 **Back in the eighties, a convention of the most powerful media magnates:** Bagdikian, 16.

108 **For a media company to survive the inevitable stinkers, it will try to distribute:** Wu, *Master Switch*, 219–21.

108 **"It is the right of the viewers and listeners, not the right of broadcasters":** Robert W. McChesney and John Nichols, *The Death and Life of American Journalism* (Nation Books, 2010), 152.

109 **When Random House bought Alfred A. Knopf in 1960:** André Schiffrin, *The Business of Books* (Verso, 2000), 1.

109 **When Time-Life, the blue whale of publishing, wanted to inhale Random House:** Bennett Cerf, *At Random* (Random House, 1977), 285.

Chapter Six: Big Tech's Smoke-Filled Room

112 **"Victorian Internet":** Tom Standage, *The Victorian Internet* (Bloomsbury, 2014), 215.

113 **The Western Union monopoly had many accomplices:** Paul Starr, *The Creation of the Media* (Basic Books, 2004), 171–73.

113 **Between 1866 and 1900, congressmen introduced seventy bills:** Starr, 176.

114 **More than 80 percent of the copy in western papers:** Menahem Blondheim, *News over the Wires* (Harvard University Press, 1994), viii.

114 **"not in any way encourage or support any opposition":** Blondheim, 151.

115 **"onerous" and "grievous" monopoly:** David Hochfelder, *The Telegraph in America, 1832–1920* (Johns Hopkins University Press, 2012), 44.

115 **"Unlike the British telegraph companies":** Starr, 177.

115 **"third rate nonentity":** Wu, *Master Switch,* 22.

116 **the organization came to be known as the "Hayesociated Press":** Starr, 187.

123 **The Harvard law professor Jonathan Zittrain has spun the following hypothetical scenario:** Jonathan Zittrain, "Facebook Could Decide an Election Without Anyone Ever Finding Out," *New Republic,* June 1, 2014.

123 **"On election night he was in our boiler room":** Joshua Green, "Google's Eric Schmidt Invests in Obama's Big Data Brains," *BloombergBusinessweek,* May 31, 2013.

124 **"Early on, [the Obama campaign] turned to Google Analytics":** "Obama for America uses Google Analytics to democratize rapid, data-driven decision making," Google Analytics Case Study, 2013.

124 **Marius Milner, an engineer at Google:** Steve Lohr and David Streitfeld, "Data Engineer in Google Case Is Identified," *New York Times,* April 30, 2012; David Streitfeld, "Google Is Faulted for Impeding U.S. Inquiry on Data Collection," *New York Times,* April 14, 2012.

125 **"On all measures, opinions shifted in the direction of the candidate who was favored":** Robert Epstein, "How Google Could Rig the 2016 Election," *Politico,* August 19, 2015; Robert Epstein and Ronald E. Robertson, "The Search Engine Manipulation Effect (SEME) and Its Possible Impact on the Outcomes of Elections," *Proceedings of the National Academy of Sciences* 112, no. 33 (August 18, 2015): E4512–21.

125 **In 1973, ads for a board game called Hüsker Dü?:** Les Brown, "Subliminal Ad Pops Up in National TV Promotion," *New York Times,* December 27, 1973.

CHAPTER SEVEN: THE VIRALITY VIRUS

132 **Companies that manufacture tchotchkes sold on Amazon:** Greg Bensinger, "Competing with Amazon on Amazon," *Wall Street Journal,* July 27, 2012.

137 **Jonah Peretti, the founder of BuzzFeed and the William Randolph Hearst of our era:** Jonah Peretti, "Mormons, Mullets, and Maniacs," New York Viral Media Meetup, August 12, 2010.

142 **"The pull of dollars towards sensationalism":** Michael Schudson, *The Sociology of News* (W. W. Norton, 2011), 73.

142 **"reign of terror" fed by a "hurricane of demagogy":** John Morton Blum, ed., *Public Philosopher: Selected Letters of Walter Lippmann* (Ticknor & Fields, 1985), 133–34.

143 **"In an exact sense the present crisis of western democracy":** Lippmann, *Liberty and the News,* 5.

143 **"We really wrote for one another. . . . We knew that no one would jump on our stories as quickly":** Robert Darnton, "Writing News and Telling Stories," *Daedalus* 104, no. 2 (Spring 1975): 175–94.

144 **Over the course of a decade, journalism shed $1.6 billion worth of reporter and editor salaries:** Taylor, 87.

144   **One survey ranked newspaper reporter as the worst job in America:** "The Worst Jobs of 2015," CareerCast.com.

145   **"A lot of what we do at BuzzFeed is give dashboards to every person":** Andy Serwer, "Inside the Mind of Jonah Peretti," *Fortune*, December 5, 2013.

146   **"Nobody wants to eat the boring vegetables. Nor does anyone want to pay to encourage people to eat their vegetables":** James Fallows, "Learning to Love the (Shallow, Divisive, Unreliable) New Media," *Atlantic*, April 2011.

147   **"The very first step, however, should be a deliberate push to abandon our current metaphors":** "Innovation," *New York Times*, March 24, 2014.

148   **"Everything looks the same, reads the same":** "Hello again," Joshua Topolsky blog, July 11, 2015.

151   **Andrew Sullivan made sport of pointing this out:** Andrew Sullivan, "Guess Which Buzzfeed Piece Is An Ad," *The Dish* blog, February 21, 2013.

CHAPTER EIGHT: DEATH OF THE AUTHOR

157   **His lectures and speeches were gripping spectacles of intellect, punctuated by multimedia:** Evan Osnos, "Embrace the Irony," *New Yorker*, October 13, 2014.

158   **One magazine profile described him as "a kind of Internet messiah":** Simon van Zuylen-Wood, "Larry Lessig, Off the Grid," *New Republic*, February 5, 2014.

158   **"Never before in the history of human culture had [creative culture] been as professionalized":** Lawrence Lessig, "Laws That Choke Creativity," TED, March 2007.

159   **"Immature poets imitate; mature poets steal":** T. S. Eliot, *Selected Essays 1917–1932* (Harcourt, Brace and Company, 1932), 182.

159   **"If communism vs. capitalism was the struggle of the twentieth century":** Taylor, 23.

159   **some of the organizations that Lessig created to advance his arguments received checks from Google:** Robert Levine, *Free Ride* (Doubleday, 2011), 84.

160   **"Amateurs are sometimes separated from professionals by skill":** Clay Shirky, *Cognitive Surplus* (Penguin, 2010), 82.

160   **"No one can succeed by themselves. . . . The only way you can achieve something":** Thomas L. Friedman, "Collaborate vs. Collaborate," *New York Times*, January 12, 2013.

161   **"God alone creates":** Thomas Aquinas, *Basic Writings of St. Thomas Aquinas*, vol. 1, ed. Anton C. Pegis (Random House, 1945), 312.

161   **Once a writer sold a manuscript, he surrendered control over it:** Mark Rose, *Authors and Owners* (Harvard University Press, 1993), 18.

162   **"I am 'sort of' haunted by the conviction":** Percy Lubbock, ed., *The Letters of Henry James: Volume 1* (Charles Scribner's Sons, 1920), 424.

163   **"Of genius the only proof is, the act of doing well what is worthy to be**

done": William Wordsworth, *The Poems of William Wordsworth* (Methuen and Co., 1908), 516.

163 **"Deny it to him, and you unfeelingly leave a weight upon his spirits"**: Martha Woodmansee and Peter Jaszi, eds., *The Construction of Authorship* (Duke University Press, 1994), 5.

164 **A reader in London would have spent about $2.50 for a copy of Dickens's *A Christmas Carol***: Siva Vaidhyanathan, *Copyrights and Copywrongs* (New York University Press, 2001), 50.

164 **By 1830, ten houses in Philadelphia alone were churning out copies of Sir Walter Scott**: Vaidhyanathan, 45.

164 **"[the] business lived to a large extent on what was morally, if not legally, thievery"**: Robert Spoo, *Without Copyrights* (Oxford University Press, 2013), 42.

165 **"I am the greatest loser by the existing Law"**: Jenny Hartley, ed., *The Selected Letters of Charles Dickens* (Oxford University Press, 2012), 96.

165 **"Because you print the stolen property aforesaid very vilely and uncleanly"**: Rudyard Kipling, *Kipling's America: Travel Letters, 1889–1895*, ed. D. H. Stewart (Johns Hopkins University Press, 2003), xx.

165 **"Few men have ever [depended on their pen for income] happily"**: Henry Holt, "The Commercialization of Literature," *Atlantic Monthly*, November 1905.

166 **"This country is being flooded with the best of English literature at prices which make a package of water closet paper"**: Frederick Anderson, Lin Salamo, Bernard L. Stein, eds., *Mark Twain's Notebooks & Journals, Volume II, 1877–1883* (University of California Press, 1975), 414.

167 **"theoretical socialist, and a practical aristocrat"**: John William Crowley, *The Dean of American Letters* (University of Massachusetts Press, 1999), 11.

167 **"It is a comfort to be right theoretically and to be ashamed of one's self practically"**: Crowley, 11.

167 **"the golden goose was found for the author"**: Holt, "Commercialization of Literature."

167 **"the one thing that always made you feel good"**: Ernest Hemingway, *Green Hills of Africa* (Scribner, 2015), 50.

167 **Fitzgerald, who described himself as a "professional" with a "protective hardness"**: James L. W. West III, ed., *F. Scott Fitzgerald, My Lost City: Personal Essays, 1920–1940* (Cambridge University Press, 2005), 189.

168 **even noting the $0.34 he received in 1929 for the English royalties of *The Great Gatsby***: William J. Quirk, "Living on $500,000 a Year," *American Scholar*, Autumn 2009.

169 **"There were just too many of us wedged onto the single bench"**: Alfred Kazin, *Starting Out in the Thirties* (Atlantic Monthly Press, 1962), 15.

170 **It found that full-time writers made a median income of about $11,000 per year**: Lewis A. Coser, Charles Kadushin, Walter W. Powell, *Books: The Culture and Commerce of Publishing* (University of Chicago Press, 1985), 233.

170 **Authors Guild's 2009 findings, which uncovered a median income of $25,000:** Authors Guild, "The Wages of Writing," 2015 Member Survey, September 2015.

171 **Turns out, a work like Beethoven's String Quartet No. 4 is a stubborn thing:** William J. Baumol and William G. Bowen, *Performing Arts* (Twentieth Century Fund, 1966).

173 **"Trade book publishing is by nature a cottage industry":** Jason Epstein, *Book Business* (W.W. Norton, 2001), 1.

174 **"In the past, the media was a full-time job. But maybe the media is going to be a part time job":** "Chris Anderson on the Economics of 'Free,'" *Der Spiegel*, July 28, 2009.

176 **"Greater technology will selfishly unleash our talents, but it will also unselfishly unleash others":** Kevin Kelly, *What Technology Wants* (Viking, 2010), 237.

177 **"The real magic will come in the second act, as each word in each book":** Kevin Kelly, "Scan This Book!," *New York Times Magazine*, May 14, 2006.

177 **"In a curious way, the universal library becomes one very, very, very large single text":** Kelly, "Scan This Book!"

177 **"By enabling people from diverse backgrounds to easily connect and share their ideas":** Evgeny Morozov, *To Save Everything, Click Here* (PublicAffairs, 2013), 292.

CHAPTER NINE: IN SEARCH OF THE ANGEL OF DATA

184 **and the Internet began its own journey to the free market:** Shane Greenstein, *How the Internet Became Commercial* (Princeton University Press, 2015). My narrative of the Internet's privatization relies heavily on Greenstein's history.

184 **forbidding "extensive use for private or personal business":** Ceruzzi, 321.

185 **"I want to create an oasis from regulation in the broadband world":** "Competition and Deregulation: Striking the Right Balance," Remarks of William E. Kennard, United States Telecom Association Annual Convention, October 18, 1999.

186 **"From somebody's hobby to somebody's industry; from jury-rigged contraption to slick production marvel":** Wu, *Master Switch*, 6.

187 **"The accumulated data can probably paint a better picture of how you spend your time":** Bruce Schneier, *Data and Goliath* (W. W. Norton, 2015), 2.

187 **"We know where you are. We know where you've been. We can more or less know what you're thinking about":** Schneier, 22.

188 **"Positive feedback makes the strong get stronger and the weak get weaker":** Carl Shapiro and Hal R. Varian, *Information Rules* (Harvard Business School Press, 1999), 175.

188 **"a God-like view of the marketplace":** Ariel Ezrachi and Maurice E. Stucke, *Virtual Competition* (Harvard University Press, 2016), 71.

189 **what he described as "the feeble judgment of the common herd":** Thurman W. Arnold, *The Folklore of Capitalism* (Beard Books, 2000), 66.

190 **"Men like Senator Borah founded political careers on the continuance of such crusades":** Arnold, 217.

190 **The Senate confirmed Arnold, although Borah allowed that Arnold should "revise that chapter on trusts":** Nomination of Thurman W. Arnold, Hearings Before a Subcommittee of the Committee on the Judiciary, United States Senate, 75th Congress, 3rd session, March 11, 1938, 5.

191 **"That debate is like arguing whether tall buildings are better than low ones":** Michael J. Sandel, *Democracy's Discontent* (Harvard University Press, 1996), 241.

191 **"Unlike antimonopolists in the tradition of Brandeis, Arnold sought not to decentralize the economy for the sake of self-government":** Sandel, 240.

191 **When the *Economist* analyzed the question last year, it found that most sectors of the economy:** "Too Much of a Good Thing," *Economist*, March 26, 2016.

191 **"markets are now more concentrated and less competitive than at any point since the Gilded Age":** K. Sabeel Rahman and Lina Khan, "Restoring Competition in the U.S. Economy," Roosevelt Institute Report, June 2016.

192 **"The final end of the State was to make men free to develop their faculties":** Jeffrey Rosen, *Louis D. Brandeis* (Yale University Press, 2016), 48.

193 **"the protection from surveillance or interference when we are engaged in the processes of generating ideas":** Neil Richards, *Intellectual Privacy* (Oxford University Press, 2015), 95.

193 **"The greatest menace to freedom is an inert people":** Rosen, 22.

194 **"The American people have as little need of oligarchy":** Louis D. Brandeis and Norman Hapgood, *Other People's Money* (F. A. Stokes, 1914), 142.

195 **Traveling Amazon employees carried misleading business cards:** Stone, 290–91.

196 **When states began collecting, household spending at Amazon dropped by 10 percent:** Robb Mandelbaum, "When Amazon Collects Sales Tax, Some Shoppers Head Elsewhere," *New York Times*, April 28, 2014.

196 **Stone described this dodging as "one of the company's biggest tactical advantages":** Stone, 287.

196 **"employing every trick in the book, and inventing many new ones":** Stone, 294.

196 **Amazon hatched Project Goldcrest:** Harry Davies and Simon Marks, "Revealed: How Project Goldcrest Helped Amazon Avoid Huge Sums in Tax," *Guardian*, February 18, 2016; Simon Marks, "Amazon: How the World's Largest Retailer Keeps Tax Collectors at Bay," *Newsweek*, July 13, 2016.

197 **Calculations by the IRS show that Project Goldcrest helped Amazon:** Davies and Marks, "Revealed"; Gaspard Sebag and David Kocieniewski, "What Is Amazon's Core Tech Worth? Depends on Which Taxman Asks," *BloombergTechnology*, August 22, 2016.

197 **By the end of 2015, it had "permanently reinvested" $58.3 billion of its profits:** "Fortune 500 Companies Hold a Record $2.4 Trillion Offshore," Citizens for Tax Justice, March 3, 2016.

197 **Facebook bilked the treasury by taking a single deduction:** "Facebook's Multi-Billion Dollar Tax Break," Citizens for Tax Justice, February 14, 2013.

197 **Walmart, the supposed Beast of Bentonville, handed over about 30 percent of its income in taxes:** David Leonhardt, "The Big Companies That Avoid Taxes," *New York Times*, October 18, 2016.

198 **Google executives set foot in the Obama White House more often than those of any other corporation:** David Dayen, "The Android Administration," *Intercept*, April 22, 2016.

198 **By one count, Google poured more into its D.C. apparatus than any other public company:** "Mission Creep-y," Public Citizen report, November 2014.

198 **"Google has achieved a kind of vertical integration with the government":** Dayen, "Android Administration."

198 **Somehow Google managed to overcome the recommendation of staffers on the Federal Trade Commission:** Brody Mullins, Rolfe Winkler, and Brent Kendall, "Inside the U.S. Antitrust Probe of Google," *Wall Street Journal*, March 19, 2015.

202 **"Assuring the public has access to a multiplicity of information sources":** McChesney and Nichols, *Death and Life*, 151.

CHAPTER TEN: THE ORGANIC MIND

206 **"fresh-frozen life in some prepackaged suburb":** Warren J. Belasco, *Appetite for Change* (Cornell University Press, 2007), 62.

206 **"Not only do they provide bread aplenty, but the bread is as soft as floss":** Belasco, 49.

207 **"White vs. brown was a central contrast. . . . Whiteness meant Wonder Bread, White Tower, Cool Whip":** Belasco, 48.

209 **"Though seldom articulated as such, the attempt to redefine, or escape, the traditional role of consumer":** Michael Pollan, "The Food Movement, Rising," *New York Review of Books*, June 10, 2010.

211 **"To overcome falling ad prices you had to redouble audience growth":** Michael Wolff, *Television Is the New Television* (Portfolio/Penguin, 2015), 50.

212 **"Websites plausibly marketed these people as members of *their* audiences":** John Herrman, "Mutually Assured Content," *The Awl*, July 30, 2015.

212 **In 2010, a site needed about ten million unique visitors per month to score a meaningful buy":** Wolff, 73.

212 "We expect that advertising-funded search engines will be inherently biased": Taylor, 184.

213 "The cost of reading, even if you buy books instead of borrowing them": George Orwell, "Books v. Cigarettes," *The Collected Essays, Journalism and Letters of George Orwell* (Harcourt, Brace & World, 1968), 94.

214 "It is not a proud record for a country which is nearly 100 per cent literate": Orwell, 95–96.

215 He used subliminal images of vaginas: Alan Bilton, *Silent Film Comedy and American Culture* (Palgrave Macmillan, 2013), 16.

215 "Propaganda," he wrote chillingly, "makes it possible for minority ideas to become effective more quickly": *Public Relations, Edward Bernays and the American Scene* (F. W. Faxon Company, 1951), 19.

215 "Where there are bookshelves, there will be books": Larry Tye, *The Father of Spin* (Henry Holt and Company, 1998), 52.

216 "the allure of propriety and abundance, which could be realized": Ted Striphas, *The Late Age of Print* (Columbia University Press, 2009), 29.

216 "We are profiting at the moment from the need for books in individual homes": Striphas, 28.

218 "*Colere* had a range of meanings: inhabit, cultivate, protect, honour with worship": Raymond Williams, *Keywords* (Oxford University Press, 1976), 87.

218 "one of the two or three most complicated words in the English language": Williams, 87.

218 the very thing that obsessed Louis Brandeis, his fixation on "developing the faculties": Rosen, 48.

219 "Taste classifies, and it classifies the classifier": Pierre Bourdieu, *Distinction* (Harvard University Press, 1984), 6.

CHAPTER ELEVEN: THE PAPER REBELLION

224 "good things don't have to be static, unchanging": Kevin Kelly, *The Inevitable* (Viking, 2016), 81.

224 "It's happening in 5 years": MG Siegler, "Nicholas Negroponte: The Physical Book Is Dead In 5 Years," *TechCrunch*, August 6, 2010.

225 In 2015, e-book revenue dropped by 11 percent: "U.S. Publishing Industry's Annual Survey Reveals Nearly $28 Billion in Revenue in 2015," Association of American Publishers, July 11, 2016.

226 As the historian Steven Roger Fischer puts it, "to read" was to read aloud: Steven Roger Fischer, *A History of Reading* (Reaktion Books, 2003), 27.

226 "Active silent reading now prevailed, which demanded engagement": Fischer, 202–3.

231 "Our very mastery seems to escape our mastery": Michel Serres, *Conversations on Science, Culture, and Time*, trans. Roxanne Lapidus (University of Michigan Press, 1995), 171–72.

Index

penguin.co.uk/vintage